W9-AFH-992

Modern Critical Interpretations

Franz Kafka's
The Castle

Modern Critical Interpretations

The Oresteia
Beowulf
The General Prologue to
  The Canterbury Tales
The Pardoner's Tale
The Knight's Tale
The Divine Comedy
Exodus
Genesis
The Gospels
The Iliad
The Book of Job
Volpone
Doctor Faustus
The Revelation of St.
  John the Divine
The Song of Songs
Oedipus Rex
The Aeneid
The Duchess of Malfi
Antony and Cleopatra
As You Like It
Coriolanus
Hamlet
Henry IV, Part I
Henry IV, Part II
Henry V
Julius Caesar
King Lear
Macbeth
Measure for Measure
The Merchant of Venice
A Midsummer Night's
  Dream
Much Ado About
  Nothing
Othello
Richard II
Richard III
The Sonnets
Taming of the Shrew
The Tempest
Twelfth Night
The Winter's Tale
Emma
Mansfield Park
Pride and Prejudice
The Life of Samuel
  Johnson
Moll Flanders
Robinson Crusoe
Tom Jones
The Beggar's Opera
Gray's Elegy
Paradise Lost
The Rape of the Lock
Tristram Shandy
Gulliver's Travels

Evelina
The Marriage of Heaven
  and Hell
Songs of Innocence and
  Experience
Jane Eyre
Wuthering Heights
Don Juan
The Rime of the Ancient
  Mariner
Bleak House
David Copperfield
Hard Times
A Tale of Two Cities
Middlemarch
The Mill on the Floss
Jude the Obscure
The Mayor of
  Casterbridge
The Return of the Native
Tess of the D'Urbervilles
The Odes of Keats
Frankenstein
Vanity Fair
Barchester Towers
The Prelude
The Red Badge of
  Courage
The Scarlet Letter
The Ambassadors
Daisy Miller, The Turn
  of the Screw, and
  Other Tales
The Portrait of a Lady
Billy Budd, Benito Cer-
  eno, Bartleby the Scriv-
  ener, and Other Tales
Moby-Dick
The Tales of Poe
Walden
Adventures of
  Huckleberry Finn
The Life of Frederick
  Douglass
Heart of Darkness
Lord Jim
Nostromo
A Passage to India
Dubliners
A Portrait of the Artist as
  a Young Man
Ulysses
Kim
The Rainbow
Sons and Lovers
Women in Love
1984
Major Barbara

Man and Superman
Pygmalion
St. Joan
The Playboy of the
  Western World
The Importance of Being
  Earnest
Mrs. Dalloway
To the Lighthouse
My Antonia
An American Tragedy
Murder in the Cathedral
The Waste Land
Absalom, Absalom!
Light in August
Sanctuary
The Sound and the Fury
The Great Gatsby
A Farewell to Arms
The Sun Also Rises
Arrowsmith
Lolita
The Iceman Cometh
Long Day's Journey Into
  Night
The Grapes of Wrath
Miss Lonelyhearts
The Glass Menagerie
A Streetcar Named
  Desire
Their Eyes Were
  Watching God
Native Son
Waiting for Godot
Herzog
All My Sons
Death of a Salesman
Gravity's Rainbow
All the King's Men
The Left Hand of
  Darkness
The Brothers Karamazov
Crime and Punishment
Madame Bovary
The Interpretation of
  Dreams
The Castle
The Metamorphosis
The Trial
Man's Fate
The Magic Mountain
Montaigne's Essays
Remembrance of Things
  Past
The Red and the Black
Anna Karenina
War and Peace

These and other titles in preparation

Modern Critical Interpretations

Franz Kafka's
The Castle

Edited and with an introduction by

Harold Bloom
Sterling Professor of the Humanities
Yale University

Chelsea House Publishers ◊ *1988*

NEW YORK ◊ NEW HAVEN ◊ PHILADELPHIA

© 1988 by Chelsea House Publishers,
a division of Chelsea House Educational Communications, Inc.

Introduction © 1988 by Harold Bloom

Printed and bound in the United States of America

10 9 8 7 6 5 4 3 2 1

∞ The paper used in this publication meets the minimum
requirements of the American National Standard for
Permanence of Paper for Printed Library Materials, Z39.48–1984

Library of Congress Cataloging-in-Publication Data
Franz Kafka's The castle / edited and with an introduction by
   Harold Bloom.
        p.   cm.—(Modern critical interpretations)
   Bibliography: p.
   Includes index.
   ISBN 1-55546-069-0 : $19.95
   1. Kafka, Franz. 1883—1924.   Schloss.   I. Bloom, Harold.
   II. Series.
PT2621.A26S399 1988
833'.912—dc 19   87-26537
                                                    CIP

Contents

Editor's Note / vii

Introduction / 1
  HAROLD BLOOM

The Caricature of Courtship / 23
  KENNETH BURKE

The Undiscover'd Country: The Death Motif
in Kafka's *Castle* / 35
  W. G. SEBALD

The Castle: To Deny Whatever Is Affirmed / 51
  RONALD GRAY

The Castle: A Company of Gnostic Demons / 81
  ERICH HELLER

Power and Authority in *The Castle* / 107
  RICHARD J. ARNESON

Texts, Textuality, and Silence in Franz Kafka's
The Castle / 125
  MARJANNE E. GOOZÉ

Chronology / 141

Contributors / 145

Bibliography / 147

Acknowledgments / 151

Index / 153

Editor's Note

This book gathers together a representative selection of the best criticism of Franz Kafka's *The Castle* that is available in English. The critical essays are reprinted here in the chronological order of their original publication. I am grateful to David Parker and Bruce Covey for their aid in editing this volume.

My introduction traces Kafka's quest for a New Kabbalah, which culminates in *The Castle,* a quest that relies upon Kafka's originality in both extending and inventing Jewish modes of Negation. Kenneth Burke, dean of living American critics, begins the chronological sequence with his reading of *The Castle* as a "caricature of courtship."

In W. G. Sebald's analysis, K.'s quest is ultimately for death. Ronald Gray's overview sees Kafka as drawing back from that final deathliness, on the verge of reversing the law that prevails in the Castle, which is to deny whatever is affirmed. In a more complex survey, Erich Heller reads Klamm and his Castle hierarchy as constituting a kind of company of Gnostic demons, blocking the land-surveyor K. from the goal of his quest.

A more political interpretation is rendered by Richard J. Arneson, who finds the pragmatic effect of the Castle's power and authority to be the powerlessness that corrupts the people in the village and begins to contaminate K., despite his resistance. In this book's final essay, Marjanne E. Goozé applies our current critical awareness of textuality to *The Castle,* asserting that "Kafka's text shows the necessity of breaking out of traditional textual systems," but evades teaching us how we are to break out.

Introduction

In her obituary for her lover, Franz Kafka, Milena Jesenská sketched a modern Gnostic, a writer whose vision was of the *kenoma,* the cosmic emptiness into which we have been thrown:

> He was a hermit, a man of insight who was frightened by life. . . . He saw the world as being full of invisible demons which assail and destroy defenseless man. . . . All his works describe the terror of mysterious misconceptions and guiltless guilt in human beings.

Milena—brilliant, fearless, and loving—may have subtly distorted Kafka's beautifully evasive slidings between normative Jewish and Jewish Gnostic stances. Max Brod, responding to Kafka's now-famous remark—"We are nihilistic thoughts that came into God's head"—explained to his friend the Gnostic notion that the Demiurge had made this world both sinful and evil. "No," Kafka replied, "I believe that we are not such a radical relapse of God's, only one of His bad moods. He had a bad day." Playing straight man, the faithful Brod asked if this meant there was hope outside our cosmos. Kafka smiled, and charmingly said: "Plenty of hope—for God—no end of hope—only not for us."

Kafka, despite Gershom Scholem's authoritative attempts to claim him for Jewish Gnosticism, is both more and less than a Gnostic, as we might expect. Yahweh can be saved, and the divine degradation that is fundamental to Gnosticism is not an element in Kafka's world. But we are fashioned out of the clay during one of Yahweh's bad moods; perhaps there was divine dyspepsia or sultry weather in the garden that Yahweh had planted in the East. Yahweh is hope, and we are hopeless. We are the jackdaws or crows, the kafkas (since that is what the name means, in Czech) whose impossibility is what the heavens signify: "The crows maintain that a single crow could destroy the heavens. Doubtless that is so, but it proves nothing against the heavens, for the heavens signify simply: the impossibility of crows."

In Gnosticism, there is an alien, wholly transcendent God, and the adept, after considerable difficulties, can find the way back to presence and fullness. Gnosticism therefore is a religion of salvation, though the most negative of all such saving visions. Kafkan spirituality offers no hope of salvation, and so is not Gnostic. But Milena Jesenská certainly was right to emphasize the Kafkan terror that is akin to Gnosticism's dread of the *kenoma,* which is the world governed by the Archons. Kafka takes the impossible step beyond Gnosticism, by denying that there is hope for us anywhere at all.

In the aphorisms that Brod rather misleadingly entitled "Reflections on Sin, Pain, Hope, and the True Way," Kafka wrote: "What is laid upon us is to accomplish the negative; the positive is already given." How much Kabbalah Kafka knew is not clear. Since he wrote a new Kabbalah, the question of Jewish Gnostic sources can be set aside. Indeed, by what seems a charming oddity (but I would call it yet another instance of Blake's insistence that forms of worship are chosen from poetic tales), our understanding of Kabbalah is Kafkan anyway, since Kafka profoundly influenced Gershom Scholem, and no one will be able to get beyond Scholem's creative or strong misreading of Kabbalah for decades to come. I repeat this point to emphasize its shock value: we read Kabbalah, via Scholem, from a Kafkan perspective, even as we read human personality and its mimetic possibilities by way of Shakespeare's perspectives, since essentially Freud mediates Shakespeare for us, yet relies upon him nevertheless. A Kafkan facticity or contingency now governs our awareness of whatever in Jewish cultural tradition is other than normative.

In his diaries for 1922, Kafka meditated, on January 16, upon "something very like a breakdown," in which it was "impossible to sleep, impossible to stay awake, impossible to endure life, or, more exactly, the course of life." The vessels were breaking for him as his demoniac, writerly inner world and the outer life "split apart, and they do split apart, or at least clash in a fearful manner." Late in the evening, K. arrives at the village, which is deep in snow. The Castle is in front of him, but even the hill upon which it stands is veiled in mist and darkness, and there is not a single light visible to show that the Castle was there. K. stands a long time on a wooden bridge that leads from the main road to the village, while gazing, not at the village, but "into the illusory emptiness above him," where the Castle should be. He does not know what he will always refuse to learn, which is that the emptiness is "illusory" in every possible sense, since he does gaze at the *kenoma,* which resulted initially from the breaking of the vessels, the splitting apart of every world, inner and outer.

Writing the vision of K., Kafka counts the costs of his confirmation, in a passage prophetic of Scholem, but with a difference that Scholem sought to negate by combining Zionism and Kabbalah for himself. Kafka knew better, perhaps only for himself, but perhaps for others as well:

> Second: This pursuit, originating in the midst of men, carries one in a direction away from them. The solitude that for the most part has been forced on me, in part voluntarily sought by me—but what was this if not compulsion too?—is now losing all its ambiguity and approaches its denouement. Where is it leading? The strongest likelihood is that it may lead to madness; there is nothing more to say, the pursuit goes right through me and rends me asunder. Or I can—can I?—manage to keep my feet somewhat and be carried along in the wild pursuit. Where, then, shall I be brought? "Pursuit," indeed, is only a metaphor. I can also say, "assault on the last earthly frontier," an assault, moreover, launched from below, from mankind, and since this too is a metaphor, I can replace it by the metaphor of an assault from above, aimed at me from above.
>
> All such writing is an assault on the frontiers; if Zionism had not intervened, it might easily have developed into a new secret doctrine, a Kabbalah. There are intimations of this. Though of course it would require genius of an unimaginable kind to strike root again in the old centuries, or create the old centuries anew and not spend itself withal, but only then begin to flower forth.

Consider Kafka's three metaphors, which he so knowingly substitutes for one another. The pursuit is of ideas, in that mode of introspection which is Kafka's writing. Yet this metaphor of pursuit is also a piercing "right through me" and a breaking apart of the self. For "pursuit," Kafka then substitutes mankind's assault, from below, on the last earthly frontier. What is that frontier? It must lie between us and the heavens. Kafka, the crow or jackdaw, by writing, transgresses the frontier and implicitly maintains that he could destroy the heavens. By another substitution, the metaphor changes to "an assault from above, aimed at me from above," the aim simply being the signifying function of the heavens, which is to mean the impossibility of Kafkas or crows. The heavens assault Kafka *through his writing;* "all such writing is an assault on the frontiers," and these must now be Kafka's own frontiers. One thinks of Freud's most complex "frontier concept," more complex even than the drive: the bodily ego. The heavens assault Kafka's bodily ego, *but only through his own writing.* Certainly such an assault is not un-Jewish, and has as much to do with normative as with esoteric Jewish tradition.

Yet, according to Kafka, his own writing, were it not for the intervention of Zionism, might easily have developed into a new Kabbalah. How are we to understand that curious statement about Zionism as the blocking agent that prevents Franz Kafka from becoming another Isaac Luria? Kafka darkly and immodestly writes: "There are intimations of this." Our teacher Gershom Scholem governs our interpretation here, of necessity. Those intimations belong to Kafka alone, or perhaps to a select few in his immediate circle. They cannot be conveyed to Jewry, even to its elite, because Zionism has taken the place of Messianic Kabbalah, including presumably the heretical Kabbalah of Nathan of Gaza, prophet of Sabbatai Zvi and of all his followers down to the blasphemous Jacob Frank. Kafka's influence upon Scholem is decisive here, for Kafka already has arrived at Scholem's central thesis of the link between the Kabbalah of Isaac Luria, the Messianism of the Sabbatarians and Frankists, and the political Zionism that gave rebirth to Israel.

Kafka goes on, most remarkably, to disown the idea that he possesses "genius of an unimaginable kind," one that either would strike root again in archaic Judaism, presumably of the esoteric sort, or more astonishingly "create the old centuries anew," which Scholem insisted Kafka had done. But can we speak, as Scholem tried to speak, of the Kabbalah of Franz Kafka? Is there a new secret doctrine in the superb stories and the extraordinary parables and paradoxes, or did not Kafka spend his genius in the act of new creation of the old Jewish centuries? Kafka certainly would have judged himself harshly as one spent withal, rather than as a writer who "only then began to flower forth."

Kafka died only two and a half years after this meditative moment, died, alas, just before his forty-first birthday. Yet as the propounder of a new Kabbalah, he had gone very probably as far as he (or anyone else) could go. No Kabbalah, be it that of Moses de Leon, Isaac Luria, Moses Cordovero, Nathan of Gaza, or Gershom Scholem, is exactly easy to interpret, but Kafka's secret doctrine, if it exists at all, is designedly uninterpretable. My working principle in reading Kafka is to observe that he did everything possible to evade interpretation, which only means that what most needs and demands interpretation in Kafka's writing is its perversely deliberate evasion of interpretation. Erich Heller's formula for getting at this evasion is: "Ambiguity has never been considered an elemental force; it is precisely this in the stories of Franz Kafka." Perhaps, but evasiveness is not the same literary quality as ambiguity.

Evasiveness is purposive; it writes between the lines, to borrow a fine trope from Leo Strauss. What does it mean when a quester for a new Negative, or perhaps rather a revisionist of an old Negative, resorts to the evasion of every possible interpretation as his central topic or theme? Kafka does not doubt guilt, but wishes to make it "possible for men to enjoy sin without guilt, almost without guilt," by reading Kafka. To enjoy sin almost without guilt is to evade interpretation, in exactly the dominant Jewish sense of interpretation. Jewish tradition, whether normative or esoteric, never teaches you to ask Nietzsche's question: "Who is the interpreter, and what power does he seek to gain over the text?" Instead, Jewish tradition asks: "Is the interpreter in the line of those who seek to build a hedge about the Torah in every age?" Kafka's power of evasiveness is not a power over his own text, and it does build a hedge about the Torah in our age. Yet no one before Kafka built up that hedge wholly out of evasiveness, not even Maimonides or Judah Halevi or even Spinoza. Subtlest and most evasive of all writers, Kafka remains the severest and most harassing of the belated sages of what will yet become the Jewish cultural tradition of the future.

II

The jackdaw or crow or Kafka is also the weird figure of the great Hunter Gracchus (whose Latin name also means a crow), who is not alive but dead, yet who floats, like one living, on his death-bark forever. When the fussy Burgomaster of Riva knits his brow, asking: "And you have no part in the other world (*das Jenseits*)?" the Hunter replies, with grand defensive irony:

> I am forever on the great stair that leads up to it. On that infinitely wide and spacious stair I clamber about, sometimes up, sometimes down, sometimes on the right, sometimes on the left, always in motion. The Hunter has been turned into a butterfly. Do not laugh.

Like the Burgomaster, we do not laugh. Being a single crow, Gracchus would be enough to destroy the heavens, but he will never get there. Instead, the heavens signify his impossibility, the absence of crows or hunters, and so he has been turned into another butterfly, which is all we can be, from the perspective of the heavens. And we bear no blame for that:

> "I had been glad to live and I was glad to die. Before I stepped aboard, I joyfully flung away my wretched load of ammunition, my knapsack, my hunting rifle that I had always been proud to carry, and I slipped into my winding sheet like a girl into her marriage dress. I lay and waited. Then came the mishap."
>
> "A terrible fate," said the Burgomaster, raising his hand defensively. "And you bear no blame for it?"
>
> "None," said the hunter. "I was a hunter; was there any sin in that? I followed my calling as a hunter in the Black Forest, where there were still wolves in those days. I lay in ambush, shot, hit my mark, flayed the skin from my victims: was there any sin in that? My labors were blessed. 'The Great Hunter of Black Forest' was the name I was given. Was there any sin in that?"
>
> "I am not called upon to decide that," said the Burgomaster, "but to me also there seems to be no sin in such things. But then, whose is the guilt?"

"The boatman's," said the Hunter. "Nobody will read what I say here, no one will come to help me; even if all the people were commanded to help me, every door and window would remain shut, everybody would take to bed and draw the bedclothes over his head, the whole earth would become an inn for the night. And there is sense in that, for nobody knows of me, and if anyone knew he would not know where I could be found, and if he knew where I could be found, he would not know how to deal with me, he would not know how to help me. The thought of helping me is an illness that has to be cured by taking to one's bed."

How admirable Gracchus is, even when compared to the Homeric heroes! They know, or think they know, that to be alive, however miserable, is preferable to being the foremost among the dead. But Gracchus wished only to be himself, happy to be a hunter when alive, joyful to be a corpse when dead: "I slipped into my winding sheet like a girl into her marriage dress." So long as everything happened in good order, Gracchus was more than content. The guilt must be the boatman's, and may not exceed mere incompetence. Being dead and yet still articulate, Gracchus is beyond help: "The thought of helping me is an illness that has to be cured by taking to one's bed."

When he gives the striking trope of the whole earth closing down like an inn for the night, with the bedclothes drawn over everybody's head, Gracchus renders the judgment: "And there is sense in that." There is sense in that only because in Kafka's world as in Freud's, or in Scholem's, or in any world deeply informed by Jewish memory, there is necessarily sense in everything, total sense, even though Kafka refuses to aid you in getting at or close to it.

But what kind of a world is that, where there is sense in everything, where everything seems to demand interpretation? There can be sense in everything, as J. H. Van den Berg once wrote against Freud's theory of repression, only if everything is already in the past and there never again can be anything wholly new. That is certainly the world of the great normative rabbis of the second century of the common era, and consequently it has been the world of most Jews ever since. Torah has been given, Talmud has risen to complement and interpret it, other interpretations in the chain of tradition are freshly forged in each generation, but the limits of Creation and of Revelation are fixed in Jewish memory. There is sense in everything because all sense is present already in the Hebrew Bible, which by definition must be totally intelligible, even if its fullest intelligibility will not shine forth until the Messiah comes.

Gracchus, hunter and jackdaw, is Kafka, pursuer of ideas and jackdaw, and the endless, hopeless voyage of Gracchus is Kafka's passage, only partly through a language not his own and largely through a life not much his own. Kafka was studying Hebrew intensively while he wrote "The Hunter Gracchus," early in 1917, and I think we may call the voyages of the dead but never-buried Gracchus a trope for Kafka's belated study of his ancestral language. He was still studying Hebrew in the spring of 1923, with his tuberculosis well advanced, and down to nearly the end he longed for Zion, dreaming of recovering his health and firmly grounding his identity by journeying to Palestine. Like Gracchus, he experienced life-in-death, though unlike Gracchus he achieved the release of total death.

"The Hunter Gracchus" as a story or extended parable is not the narrative of a Wandering Jew or Flying Dutchman, because Kafka's trope for his writing activity is not so much a wandering or even a wavering, but rather a repetition, labyrinthine and burrow-building. His writing repeats not itself, but a Jewish esoteric interpretation of Torah that Kafka himself scarcely knows, or even needs to know. What this interpretation tells Kafka is that there is no written Torah but only an oral one. However, Kafka has no one to tell him what this Oral Torah is. He substitutes his own writing therefore for the Oral Torah not made available to him. He is precisely in the stance of the Hunter Gracchus, who concludes by saying, " 'I am here, more than that I do not know, further than that I cannot go. My ship has no rudder, and it is driven by the wind that blows in the undermost regions of death.' "

III

"What is the Talmud if not a message from the distance?" Kafka wrote to Robert Klopstock, on December 19, 1923. What was all of Jewish tradition, to Kafka, except a message from an endless distance? That is surely part of the burden of the famous parable "An

Imperial Message," which concludes with you, the reader, sitting at your window when evening falls and dreaming to yourself the parable—that God, in his act of dying, has sent you an individual message. Heinz Politzer read this as a Nietzschean parable, and so fell into the trap set by the Kafkan evasiveness:

> Describing the fate of the parable in a time depleted of metaphysical truths, the imperial message has turned into the subjective fantasy of a dreamer who sits at a window with a view on a darkening world. The only real information imported by this story is the news of the Emperor's death. This news Kafka took over from Nietzsche.

No, for even though you dream the parable, the parable conveys truth. The Talmud does exist; it really is an Imperial message from the distance. The distance is too great; it cannot reach you; there is hope, but not for you. Nor is it so clear that God is dead. He is always dying, yet always whispers a message into the angel's ear. It is said to you that: "Nobody could fight his way through here even with a message from a dead man," but the Emperor actually does not die in the text of the parable.

Distance is part of Kafka's crucial notion of the Negative, which is not a Hegelian nor a Heideggerian Negative, but is very close to Freud's Negation and also to the Negative imaging carried out by Scholem's Kabbalists. But I want to postpone Kafka's Jewish version of the Negative until later. "The Hunter Gracchus" is an extraordinary text, but it is not wholly characteristic of Kafka at his strongest, at his uncanniest or most sublime.

When he is most himself, Kafka gives us a continuous inventiveness and originality that rivals Dante and truly challenges Proust and Joyce as that of the dominant Western author of our century, setting Freud aside, since Freud ostensibly is science and not narrative or mythmaking, though if you believe that, then you can be persuaded of anything. Kafka's beast fables are rightly celebrated, but his most remarkable fabulistic being is neither animal nor human, but is little Odradek, in the curious sketch, less than a page and a half long, "The Cares of a Family Man," where the title might have been translated "The Sorrows of a Paterfamilias." The family man narrates these five paragraphs, each a dialectical lyric in itself, beginning with one that worries the meaning of the name:

Some say the word Odradek is of Slavonic origin, and try to account for it on that basis. Others again believe it to be of German origin, only influenced by Slavonic. The uncertainty of both interpretations allows one to assume with justice that neither is accurate, especially as neither of them provides an intelligent meaning of the word.

This evasiveness was overcome by the scholar Wilhelm Emrich, who traced the name Odradek to the Czech word *odraditi,* meaning to dissuade anyone from doing anything. Like Edward Gorey's Doubtful Guest, Odradek is uninvited yet will not leave, since implicitly he dissuades you from doing anything about his presence, or rather something about his very uncanniness advises you to let him alone:

No one, of course, would occupy himself with such studies if there were not a creature called Odradek. At first glance it looks like a flat star-shaped spool for thread, and indeed it does seem to have thread wound upon it; to be sure, they are only old, broken-off bits of thread, knotted and tangled together, of the most varied sorts and colors. But it is not only a spool, for a small wooden crossbar sticks out of the middle of the star, and another small rod is joined to that at a right angle. By means of this latter rod on one side and one of the points of the star on the other, the whole thing can stand upright as if on two legs.

Is Odradek a "thing," as the bemused family man begins by calling him, or is he not a childlike creature, a daemon at home in the world of children? Odradek clearly was made by an inventive and humorous child, rather in the spirit of the making of Adam out of the moistened red clay by the J writer's Yahweh. It is difficult not to read Odradek's creation as a deliberate parody when we are told that "the whole thing can stand upright as if on two legs," and again when the suggestion is ventured that Odradek, like Adam, "once had some sort of intelligible shape and is now only a broken-down remnant." If Odradek is fallen, he is still quite jaunty, and cannot be closely scrutinized, since he "is extraordinarily nimble and can never be laid hold of," like the story in which he appears. Odradek not only advises you not to do anything about him, but in some clear sense he is yet another figure by means of whom Kafka advises you against interpreting Kafka.

One of the loveliest moments in all of Kafka comes when you, the paterfamilias, encounter Odradek leaning directly beneath you against the banisters. Being inclined to speak to him, as you would to a child, you receive a surprise: " 'Well, what's your name?' you ask him. 'Odradek,' he says. 'And where do you live?' 'No fixed abode,' he says and laughs; but it is only the kind of laughter that has no lungs behind it. It sounds rather like the rustling of fallen leaves."

"The 'I' is another," Rimbaud once wrote, adding: "So much the worse for the wood that finds it is a violin." So much the worse for the wood that finds it is Odradek. He laughs at being a vagrant, if only by the bourgeois definition of having "no fixed abode," but the laughter, not being human, is uncanny. And so he provokes the family man to an uncanny reflection, which may be a Kafkan parody of Freud's death drive beyond the pleasure principle:

> I ask myself, to no purpose, what is likely to happen to him? Can he possibly die? Anything that dies has had some kind of aim in life, some kind of activity, which has worn out; but that does not apply to Odradek. Am I to suppose, then, that he will always be rolling down the stairs, with ends of thread trailing after him, right before the feet of my children? He does no harm to anyone that I can see, but the idea that he is likely to survive me I find almost painful.

The aim of life, Freud says, is death, is the return of the organic to the inorganic, supposedly our earlier state of being. Our activity wears out, and so we die because, in an uncanny sense, we wish to die. But Odradek, harmless and charming, is a child's creation, aimless, and so not subject to the death drive. Odradek is immortal, being daemonic, and he represents also a Freudian return of the repressed, of something repressed in the *paterfamilias,* something from which the family man is in perpetual flight. Little Odradek is precisely what Freud calls a cognitive return of the repressed, while (even as) a complete affective repression is maintained. The family man introjects Odradek intellectually, but totally projects him affectively. Odradek, I now suggest, is best understood as Kafka's synecdoche for *Verneinung;* Kafka's version (not altogether un-Freudian) of Jewish Negation, a version I hope to adumbrate in what follows.

IV

Why does Kafka have so unique a spiritual authority? Perhaps the question should be rephrased. What kind of spiritual authority does Kafka have for us, or why are we moved or compelled to read him as one who has such authority? Why invoke the question of authority at all? Literary authority, however we define it, has no necessary relation to spiritual authority, and to speak of a spiritual authority in Jewish writing anyway always has been to speak rather dubiously. Authority is not a Jewish concept but a Roman one, and so makes perfect contemporary sense in the context of the Roman Catholic Church, but little sense in Jewish matters, despite the squalors of Israeli politics and the flaccid pieties of American Jewish nostalgias. There is no authority without hierarchy, and hierarchy is not a very Jewish concept either. We do not want the rabbis, or anyone else, to tell us what or who is not Jewish. The masks of the normative conceal not only the eclecticism of Judaism and of Jewish culture, but also the nature of the J writer's Yahweh himself. It is absurd to think of Yahweh as having mere authority. He is no Roman godling who augments human activities, nor a Homeric god helping to constitute an audience for human heroism.

Yahweh is neither a founder nor an onlooker, though sometimes he can be mistaken for either or both. His essential trope is fatherhood rather than foundation, and his interventions are those of a covenanter rather than of a spectator. You cannot found an authority upon him, because his benignity is manifested not through augmentation but through creation. He does not write; he speaks and he is heard in time, and what he continues to create by his speaking is *olam,* time without boundaries, which is more than just an augmentation. More of anything else can come through authority, but more life is the blessing itself, and comes, beyond authority, to Abraham, to Jacob, and to David. No more than Yahweh, do any of them have mere authority. Yet Kafka certainly does have literary authority, and in a troubled way his literary authority is now spiritual also, particularly in Jewish contexts. I do not think that this is a post-Holocaust phenomenon, though Jewish Gnosticism, oxymoronic as it may or may not be, certainly seems appropriate to our time, to many among us. Literary Gnosticism does not seem to me a time-bound phenomenon, anyway. Kafka's *The Castle,* as Erich Heller has argued, is clearly more Gnostic than normative in its spiritual temper, but then so is Shakespeare's *Macbeth,* and Blake's *The Four Zoas,* and Carlyle's *Sartor Resartus.* We sense a Jewish element in Kafka's apparent Gnosticism, even if we are less prepared than Scholem was to name it as a new Kabbalah. In his 1922 diaries, Kafka subtly insinuated that even his espousal of the Negative was dialectical:

> The Negative alone, however strong it may be, cannot suffice, as in my unhappiest moments I believe it can. For if I have gone the tiniest step upward, won any, be it the most dubious kind of security for myself, I then stretch out on my step and wait for the Negative, not to climb up to me, indeed, but to drag me down from it. Hence it is a defensive instinct in me that won't tolerate my having the slightest degree of lasting ease and smashes the marriage bed, for example, even before it has been set up.

What is the Kafkan Negative, whether in this passage or elsewhere? Let us begin by dismissing the Gallic notion that there is anything Hegelian about it, any more than there is anything Hegelian about the Freudian *Verneinung.* Kafka's Negative, unlike Freud's, is uneasily and remotely descended from the ancient tradition of negative theology, and perhaps even from that most negative of ancient theologies, Gnosticism, and yet Kafka, despite his yearnings for transcendence, joins Freud in accepting the ultimate authority of the fact. The given suffers no destruction in Kafka or in Freud, and this given essentially is the way things are, for everyone, and for the Jews in particular. If fact is supreme, then the mediation of the Hegelian Negative becomes an absurdity, and no destructive use of such a Negative is possible, which is to say that Heidegger becomes impossible, and Derrida, who is a strong misreading of Heidegger, becomes quite unnecessary.

The Kafkan Negative most simply is his Judaism, which is to say the spiritual form of Kafka's self-conscious Jewishness, as exemplified in that extraordinary aphorism: "What is laid upon us is to accomplish the negative; the positive is already given." The positive here is the Law or normative Judaism; the negative is not so much Kafka's new Kabbalah as it is that which is still laid upon us: the Judaism of the Negative, of the future as it is always rushing towards us.

His best biographer to date, Ernst Pawel, emphasizes Kafka's consciousness "of his identity as a Jew, not in the religious, but in the national sense." Still, Kafka was not a Zionist, and perhaps he longed not so much for Zion as for a Jewish language, be it Yiddish or Hebrew. He could not see that his astonishing stylistic purity in German was precisely his way of *not* betraying his self-identity as a Jew. In his final phase, Kafka thought of going to Jerusalem, and again intensified his study of Hebrew. Had he lived, he would probably have gone to Zion, perfected a vernacular Hebrew, and given us the bewilderment of Kafkan parables and stories in the language of the J writer and of Judah Halevi.

V

What calls out for interpretation in Kafka is his refusal to be interpreted, his evasiveness even in the realm of his own Negative. Two of his most beautifully enigmatical performances, both late, are the parable "The Problem of Our Laws" and the story or testament "Josephine the Singer and the Mouse Folk." Each allows a cognitive return of Jewish cultural memory, while refusing the affective identification that would make either parable or tale specifically Jewish in either historical or contemporary identification. "The Problem of Our Laws" is set as a problem in the parable's first paragraph:

> Our laws are not generally known; they are kept secret by the small group of nobles who rule us. We are convinced that these ancient laws are scrupulously administered; nevertheless it is an extremely painful thing to be ruled by laws that one does not know. I am not thinking of possible discrepancies that may arise in the interpretation of the laws, or of the disadvantages involved when only a few and not the whole people are allowed to have a say in their interpretation. These disadvantages are perhaps of no great importance. For the laws are very ancient; their interpretation has been the work of centuries, and has itself doubtless acquired the status of law; and though there is still a possible freedom of interpretation left, it has now become very restricted. Moreover the nobles have obviously no cause to be influenced in their interpretation by

personal interests inimical to us, for the laws were made to the advantage of the nobles from the very beginning, they themselves stand above the laws, and that seems to be why the laws were entrusted exclusively into their hands. Of course, there is wisdom in that—who doubts the wisdom of the ancient laws?—but also hardship for us; probably that is unavoidable.

In Judaism, the Law is precisely what is generally known, proclaimed, and taught by the normative sages. The Kabbalah was secret doctrine, but increasingly was guarded not by the normative rabbis, but by Gnostic sectaries, Sabbatarians, and Frankists, all of them ideologically descended from Nathan of Gaza, Sabbatai Zvi's prophet. Kafka twists askew the relation between normative and esoteric Judaism, again making a synecdochal representation impossible. It is not the rabbis or normative sages who stand above the Torah but the *minim,* the heretics from Elisha Ben Abuyah through to Jacob Frank, and in some sense, Gershom Scholem as well. To these Jewish Gnostics, as the parable goes on to insinuate: "The Law is whatever the nobles do." So radical a definition tells us "that the tradition is far from complete," and that a kind of Messianic expectation is therefore necessary.

This view, so comfortless as far as the present is concerned, is lightened only by the belief that a time will eventually come when the tradition and our research into it will jointly reach their conclusion, and as it were gain a breathing space, when everything will have become clear, the law will belong to the people, and the nobility will vanish.

If the parable at this point were to be translated into early Christian terms, then "the nobility" would be the Pharisees, and "the people" would be the Christian believers. But Kafka moves rapidly to stop such a translation: "This is not maintained in any spirit of hatred against the nobility; not at all, and by no one. We are more inclined to hate ourselves, because we have not yet shown ourselves worthy of being entrusted with the laws."

"We" here cannot be either Christians or Jews. Who then are those who "have not yet shown ourselves worthy of being entrusted with the laws"? They would appear to be the crows or jackdaws again, a Kafka or a Hunter Gracchus, wandering about in a state perhaps vulnerable to self-hatred or self-distrust, waiting for a Torah that will not be revealed. Audaciously, Kafka then concludes with overt paradox:

> Actually one can express the problem only in a sort of paradox: Any party that would repudiate not only all belief in the laws, but the nobility as well, would have the whole people behind it; yet no such party can come into existence, for nobody would dare to repudiate the nobility. We live on this razor's edge. A writer once summed the matter up in this way: The sole visible and indubitable law that is imposed upon us is the nobility, and must we ourselves deprive ourselves of that one law?

Why would no one dare to repudiate the nobility, whether we read them as normative Pharisees, Jewish Gnostic heresiarchs, or whatever? Though imposed upon us, the sages *or* the *minim* are the only visible evidence of law that we have. Who are we then? How is the parable's final question, whether open or rhetorical, to be answered? "Must we ourselves deprive ourselves of that one law?" Blake's answer in *The Marriage of Heaven and Hell* was: "One Law for the Lion and the Ox is Oppression." But what is one law for the crows? Kafka will not tell us whether it is oppression or not.

Josephine the singer also is a crow or Kafka, rather than a mouse, and the folk may be interpreted as an entire nation of jackdaws. The spirit of the Negative, dominant if uneasy in "The Problem of Our Laws," is loosed into a terrible freedom in Kafka's testamentary story. That is to say: in the parable, the laws could not be Torah, though that analogue flickered near. But in Josephine's story, the mouse folk simultaneously are *and* are not the Jewish people, and Franz Kafka both is *and* is not their curious singer. Cognitively the identifications are possible, as though returned from forgetfulness, but affectively they certainly are not, unless we can assume that crucial aspects making up the identifications have been purposefully, if other than consciously, forgotten. Josephine's piping *is* Kafka's story, and yet Kafka's story is hardly Josephine's piping.

Can there be a mode of negation neither conscious nor unconscious, neither Hegelian nor Freudian? Kafka's genius provides one, exposing many shades between consciousness and the work of repression, many demarcations far ghostlier than we could have imagined without him. Perhaps the ghostliest come at the end of the story:

> Josephine's road, however, must go downhill. The time will soon come when her last notes sound and die into silence. She is a small episode in the eternal history of our people, and the people will get over the loss of her. Not that it will be easy for us; how can our gatherings take place in utter silence? Still, were they not silent even when Josephine was present? Was her actual piping notably louder and more alive than the memory of it will be? Was it even in her lifetime more than a simple memory? Was it not rather because Josephine's singing was already past losing in this way that our people in their wisdom prized it so highly?
>
> So perhaps we shall not miss so very much after all, while Josephine, redeemed from the earthly sorrows which to her thinking lay in wait for all chosen spirits, will happily lose herself in the numberless throng of the heroes of our people, and soon, since we are no historians, will rise to the heights of redemption and be forgotten like all her brothers.

"I am a Memory come alive," Kafka wrote in the diaries. Whether or not he intended it, he was Jewish memory come alive. "Was it even in her lifetime more than a simple memory?" Kafka asks, knowing that he too was past losing. The Jews are no historians, in some sense, because Jewish memory, as Yosef Yerushalmi has demonstrated, is a normative mode and not a historical one. Kafka, if he could have prayed, might have prayed to rise to the heights of redemption and be forgotten like most of his brothers and sisters. But his prayer would not have been answered. When we think of *the* Catholic writer, we think of Dante, who nevertheless had the audacity to enshrine his Beatrice in the hierarchy of Paradise. If we think of *the* Protestant writer, we think of Milton, a party or sect of one, who believed that the soul was mortal, and would be resurrected only in conjunction with the body. Think of *the* Jewish writer, and you must think of Kafka, who evaded his own audacity, and believed nothing, and trusted only in the Covenant of being a writer.

VI

The full-scale instance of Kafka's new Negative or new Kabbalah is *The Castle,* an unfinished and unfinishable autobiographical novel which is the story of K., the land-surveyor. What is written between its lines? Assaulting the last earthly frontier, K. is necessarily audacious, but if what lies beyond the frontier is represented ultimately by Klamm, an imprisoning silence, lord of the *kenoma* or cosmic emptiness, then no audacity can suffice. You cannot redraw the frontiers, even if the authorities desired this, when you arrive at the administrative center of a catastrophe creation, where the demarcations hold fast against a supposed chaos or abyss, which is actually the negative emblem of the truth that the false or marred creation refuses. *The Castle* is the tale of how Kafka cannot write his way back to the abyss, of how K. cannot do his work as land-surveyor.

Part of K.'s burden is that he is not audacious enough, even though audacity could not be enough anyway. Here is the interpretive audacity of Erich Heller, rightly rejecting all those who identify the Castle with spirituality and authentic grace, but himself missing the ineluctable evasiveness of Kafka's new Kabbalah:

> The Castle of Kafka's novel is, as it were, the heavily fortified garrison of a company of Gnostic demons, successfully holding an advanced position against the maneuvers of an impatient soul. There is no conceivable idea of divinity which could justify those interpreters who see in the Castle the residence of "divine law and divine grace." Its officers are totally indifferent to good if they are not positively wicked. Neither in their decrees nor in their activities is there any trace of love, mercy, charity, or majesty. In their icy detachment they inspire certainly no awe, but fear and revulsion. Their servants are a plague to the village, "a wild, unmanageable lot, ruled by their insatiable impulses . . . their scandalous behavior knows no limits," an anticipation of the blackguards who were to become the footmen of European dictators rather than the office boys of a divine ministry. Compared to the petty and apparently calculated torture of this tyranny, the gods of Shakespeare's indignation who "kill us for their sport" are at least majestic in their wantonness.

On such a reading, Klamm would be the Demiurge, leader of a company of Archons, gods of this world. Kafka is too evasive and too negative to give us so positive and simplistic an account of triumphant evil, or at least of reigning indifference to the good. Such Gnostic symbolism would make Klamm and his cohorts representatives of ignorance, and K. in contrast a knower, but K. knows almost nothing, particularly about his own self, and from the start overestimates his own strength even as he deceives himself into the belief that the Castle underestimates him. The Castle is there primarily because K. is ignorant, though K.'s deepest drive is for knowledge. K.'s largest error throughout is his desire for a personal confrontation with Klamm, which necessarily is impossible. K., the single crow or jackdaw, would be sufficient to destroy the authority of Klamm, but Klamm and the Castle of Westwest signify simply the absence of crows, the inability of K. to achieve knowledge and therefore the impossibility of K. himself, the failure of land-surveying or of assaulting the frontiers, of writing a new Kabbalah.

Klamm is named by Wilhelm Emrich as the interpersonal element in the erotic, which seems to me just as subtle an error as judging Klamm to be the Demiurge, leader of a company of Gnostic demons. It might be more accurate to call Klamm the impersonal element in the erotic, the drive, as Martin Greenberg does, yet even that identification is evaded by Kafka's text. Closer to Klamm, as should be expected, is the negative aspect of the drive, its entropy, whose effect upon consciousness is nihilistic. Freud, in his posthumous *An Outline of Psychoanalysis* (1940) says of the drives that "they represent the somatic demands upon mental life." That approximates Klamm, but only if you give priority to Thanatos over Eros, to the death drive over sexuality. Emrich, a touch humorlessly, even identifies Klamm with Eros, which would give us a weird Eros indeed:

> Accordingly, then, Klamm is the "power" that brings the lovers together as well as the power which, bestowing happiness and bliss, is present within love itself. K. seeks contact with this power, sensing its proximity in love, a proximity great enough for communicating in whispers; but he must "manifest" such communication and contact with this power itself through a spiritual–intellectual ex-

pression of his own; this means that, as an independent spiritual-intellectual being, he must confront this power eye to eye, as it were; he must "manifest" to this super-personal power his own understanding, his own relation with it, a relation "known" only to him at the present time; that means, he must make this relation known to the power as well.

Emrich seems to found this equation on the love affair between K. and Frieda, which begins, in famous squalor, on the floor of a bar:

Fortunately Frieda soon came back; she did not mention K., she only complained about the peasants, and in the course of looking round for K. went behind the counter, so that he was able to touch her foot. From that moment he felt safe. Since Frieda made no reference to K., however, the landlord was compelled to do it. "And where is the Land-Surveyor?" he asked. He was probably courteous by nature, refined by constant and relatively free intercourse with men who were much his superior, but there was remarkable consideration in his tone to Frieda, which was all the more striking because in his conversation he did not cease to be an employer addressing a servant, and a saucy servant at that. "The Land-Surveyor—I forgot all about him," said Frieda, setting her small foot on K.'s chest. "He must have gone out long ago." "But I haven't seen him," said the landlord, "and I was in the hall nearly the whole time." "Well, he isn't in here," said Frieda coolly. "Perhaps he's hidden somewhere," said the landlord. "From the impression I had of him, he's capable of a good deal." "He would hardly dare to do that," said Frieda, pressing her foot down on K. There was a certain mirth and freedom about her which K. had not previously noticed, and quite unexpectedly it took the upper hand, for suddenly laughing she bent down to K. with the words: "Perhaps he's hidden underneath here," kissed him lightly, and sprang up again saying with a troubled air: "No, he's not there." Then the landlord, too, surprised K. when he said: "It bothers me not to know for certain that he's gone. Not only because of Herr Klamm, but because of the rule of the house. And the rule applies to you, Fräulein Frieda, just as much as to me. Well, if you answer for the bar, I'll go through the rest of the rooms. Good night! Sleep well!" He could hardly have left the room before Frieda had turned out the electric light and was under the counter beside K. "My darling! My darling!" she whispered, but she did not touch him. As if swooning with love, she lay on her back and stretched out her arms; time must have seemed endless to her in the prospect of her happiness, and she sighed rather than sang some little song or other. Then as K. still lay absorbed in thought, she started up and began to tug at him like a child. "Come on, it's too close down here," and they embraced each other, her little body burned in K.'s hands, in a state of unconsciousness which K. tried again and again but in vain to master they rolled a little way, landing with a thud on Klamm's door, where they lay among the small puddles of beer and other refuse scattered on the floor.

"Landing with a thud on Klamm's door" is Kafka's outrageously rancid trope for a successful completion to copulation, but that hardly makes Klamm into a benign Eros, with his devotees lying "among the small puddles of beer and other refuse scattered on the floor." One could recall the libertines among the Gnostics, ancient and modern, who seek to redeem the sparks upwards by a redemption *through* sin. Frieda, faithful disciple and former mistress of Klamm, tells K. that she believes it is Klamm's "doing that we came together there under the counter; blessed, not cursed, be the hour." Emrich gives full credence to Frieda, a rather dangerous act for an exegete, and certainly K. desperately believes Frieda, but then, as Heller remarks, "K. loves Frieda—if he loves her at all—entirely for Klamm's sake." That K., despite his drive for freedom, may be deceived as to Klamm's nature is understandable, but I do not think that Kafka was deceived or wished to be deceived. If Klamm is to be identified, it ought to be with what is silent, imprisoned, and unavailable in copulation, something that partakes of the final Negative, the drive towards death.

Whether *The Castle* is of the aesthetic eminence of Kafka's finest stories, parables, and fragments is open to considerable doubt, but *The Castle* is certainly the best text for studying Kafka's Negative, his hidden and subversive New Kabbalah. It abides as the most enigmatic major novel of our century, and one sees why Kafka himself thought it a failure. But all Kabbalah—old and new—has to fail when it offers itself openly to more than a handful. Perhaps *The Castle* fails as the *Zohar* fails, but like the *Zohar*, Kafka's *Castle* will go on failing from one era to another.

The Caricature of Courtship

Kenneth Burke

Thomas Mann calls Kafka "a religious humorist." A good formula, so good that it deserves a fuller explanation than the one its originator gives for it. Mann sees in Kafka the shift between love of the commonplace and desire "to be near to God, to live in God, to live aright and after God's will." And as in Mann's *Tonio Kröger* an unresolved conflict between artistic and bourgeois motives leads to sentiment and humor, so Mann says that the motives responsible for *The Castle* "correspond in the religious sphere to Tonio Kröger's isolation."

But even in *Tonio Kröger,* as viewed from the standpoint of our concern with the magic of courtship, we should note that there is a pronounced concern with *caste.* Tonio's shy reverence for the bourgeois Ingeborg is but a localization, in sexual terms, of a nostalgic attitude towards the bourgeoisie as a class. True, as the returns have kept coming in, we have begun to see that the artistic "break-away," the bourgeois-turned-Bohemian, was not so antithetical to the motives of his class as he usually felt himself to be. The young Bohemian's wandering is but the first stage of the old Bohemian's homecoming. The Bohemian is "substantially" back before he leaves; but as with the Boyg's instructions to Peer Gynt, he must get there roundabout. Still, however indistinguishable the father and the prodigal son may be as regards their underlying community of motives, they can feel themselves as opposite extremes, as different in *kind*—and Mann's story got much poignancy from the distinction between the practical-bourgeois and the esthetic-bourgeois, treated as alien *classes,* with Tonio vacillating between them, and the two women, Ingeborg and Lizaveta, being courted not merely for themselves alone, but for the contrasting orders of social motives which they represented. They were mysterious vessels, for they were sexual embodiments of two nonsexual principles, two different castes. And the ambiguous courting of them was a roundabout intercourse between the castes.

If you substitute the religious motive for the esthetic motive, you see that Mann is quite correct in noting a motivational analogy between *The Castle* and *Tonio Kröger.* But for our purposes, the significant element of the analogy was omitted from Mann's account of his own story. Add this element, and if you then look at Kafka's novel with the dialectic of *The Courtier* in mind, you will see exactly why and how Mann's formula fits. Kafka is, if you will, "religious" in his concern with the ultimate mystery, the universal ground of human motives. But his account of the religious motive is "humorous" because he never forgets how the terms of the social order incongruously shape our idea of God, inviting men to conceive of communication with God after the analogy of their worldly embarrassments.

The principle of courtship is manifested in Expressionistically grotesque fragments. It is there, because the theme is bureaucracy, communication between higher and lower orders, involving the mysteries of "reverence." And since the ultimate of such courtship would be communion between lowly beings and "the highest," Kafka goes to the very essence of his subject, seeing through social mystery to divine mystery. But he never forgets, or lets us forget, the disproportion between social mystery and divine mystery. Thus, though the social mystery provides an imagery for figuring the divine mystery, this imagery is absurdly incommensurate with the hierarchic principle in its ultimate reaches.

In Kafka's personal case, of course, the social mystery was experienced, and suffered, in the form of anti-Semitism. The Jew in liberal, pre-Hitlerite Austria was never quite blackballed, never quite admitted. Where much liberalism prevailed even while the movement towards Nazism was taking form, the Jew's social status was unsettled. And this extraliterary situation had its analogue in the plot

of *The Castle,* notably the uncertainty whether his principal character, "K.," would strengthen or lose his contacts with the Castle.
(Similarly, in *The Trial,* there was uncertainty whether K. would be
pronounced innocent or guilty by a mysterious court that was
nowhere and everywhere; indeed, he could not even learn what the
charge against him was.)

To an extent, the condition was like being blackballed, flatly
excluded from participation in the mysteries of status. Yet to an
extent it was like being hazed. For though hazing is a trial, the
"guilty" defendant may hope for eventual admission into the inner
sanctum, the holy of holies. The candidate who is being hazed can
hope to become an *insider,* even while he undergoes ritual punishments that impress upon him his nature as a partial *outsider.* Or
rather, the situation is like that of "exclusive" schools where the
upper classmen impose menial duties upon the newcomers; or it is
like hierarchic codes for imparting mystery to fraternities and secret
orders. No, there is one important difference: usually, where such
rituals prevail, they are recognized formally, so that, even while the
discomfitures build up as much "reverence" as the dingy institution
can command, the candidate knows where he is, knows what acts
will finally permit him to become one with the mystic substance.
But where there are no such formal fixities, the situation is not
recognized for what it is. Though the candidate is being hazed,
neither he nor his persecutors recognize what is going on. Hence,
nobody is quite sure what the defendant's "guilt" is, or what kind of
"trial" he must face, or for what purpose.

Thus, a friend said: "After the financial crash of 1929, you will
remember, there was a great rush of liberal intellectuals to join the
cause of political radicalism. Of a sudden, radical literacy organizations which had been struggling along for years were overwhelmed
with new converts. Whereas the old-timers in these organizations
had been laboriously attempting to increase the membership, the
situation now became reversed. Instead of a welcome for the new
men, there was a tendency to prove that they were poor material.
And this tendency went so far that often, rather than being propa-
gandists who delighted in the growth of their cause, the old-timers
acted like residents of an exclusive neighborhood who resented a
new real-estate development nearby.

"Years after, I understood what was wrong. It was not just that
the old-timers feared for the loss of their former influence in the

organization. It was the careless trampling on the mystery that disturbed them. The new men came in like a troop of boys entering a restaurant. There were no stages, there were no punishments, there was no hazing. At one moment, they weren't there, and at the next moment of a sudden they were. And lacking any formal ritual designed for this situation, the old-timers unbeknownst to themselves worked out a kind of informal hazing process, or tried to, in seeking to freeze out the very persons whom formerly they would have worked like demons to recruit."

For the Jew Kafka, the hazing that would reaffirm the mystery was not formalized. Indeed, there was not even the assurance that he was being considered. As the novelist says of one ostracized character in *The Castle,* his superiors couldn't forgive him, because they hadn't accused him; and "before he could be forgiven he had to prove his guilt." Still further, there was no clear hint as to where the mystery was, or what it was. The nearest visible, formal signs of it were in the structure of bureaucracy. Giving it maximum resonance, one got to the connotations of "God," hence one was "religious"; but realizing how inadequate it was as a figuring of the divine, one treated it with grotesque "humor." Thus, the mysterious official whose substance comes not from his intrinsic personality but solely from the dignity of his office here takes on a new dimension. He is a nonentity in the sense that he manifests no *intrinsic properties* fitting him to represent the religious motive; yet the mysteries of rank endow him with "reverence" anyhow. Indeed, his very unfitness as a vicar perversely suggests the dignifying effect of the office itself. (Thus a student wholly impressed with his college as a mystery would manifest this essence not through learning, but through a "college spirit" that would forgo learning. Or a man of means who distributed insults along with his funds, purchasing services solely through his money, beating his dogs with a bone, might more forcefully illustrate the power of money in its "purity" than if he also had appealing traits of character that engaged people's loyalties.) So in *The Castle* the very dinginess of the officialdom as *persons* absurdly suggests the omnipresence of the mystery that infuses their *office*.

Since, according to our view, *The Castle* is a fragmentary caricature of such an order, let us see to what extent the formal elements in Castiglione's dialogue have their grotesque counterpart in Kafka's novel.

The first concern of *The Courtier* is with the qualifications that make one presentable at court, and with the hopes of favor and advancement at the hands of the sovereign. This is also the primary concern of the land-surveyor, K. But whereas the courtier is concerned with the procuring of advantage *within* the court, K. is wholly an outsider, with a vast officialdom (the grotesque bureaucratic equivalent of the courtiers) vaguely interposed between him and the mysterious sovereign. K. is at several removes from the source of favor. He is a stranger among the villagers. Though the villagers belong to the castle, there is a gulf between them and the castle. There are messengers (the grotesque counterpart of angels) who live in the village but have access to outer offices in the castle. And there are the officials themselves, who represent the castle in the village, but are so imbued with the mystic standoffishness of hierarchy that throughout the entire novel K. exhausts himself in unsuccessful attempts to get preparatory interviews with them. Where the courtier can consider how one should conduct oneself in the lord's secret chamber, K. must worry how to get beyond the outer vestibule.

Frieda and Amalia are the main translations of the grotesque courtliness into terms of woman. Of Frieda, we are told: "It was her nearness to Klamm" (she had been his mistress before coming to live with K.) "that made her so irrationally seductive" to K.—and Klamm was the official from the castle whom K. is constantly striving to meet in behalf of his nightmarishly indeterminate cause. Amalia is the girl whose life was ruined when she resented a letter from an official making filthy proposals to her (a letter couched in the language of courtship incongruously reversed). One character quotes a local saying, "Official decisions are as shy as young girls"; the novelist here ingeniously mixes the sexual and bureaucratic orders. And when Kafka is contrasting "the power, merely formal until now, which Klamm exercised over K.'s services" with "the very real power which Klamm possessed in K.'s bedroom," he says: "Never yet had K. seen vocation and life so interlaced as here. . . . One might think that they had exchanged places."

If we recall what we previously said on the relation between mystery and class, this remark seems unusually resonant. Status and division of labor being but two aspects of the same thing, the reference to "vocation" can be read as a roundabout reference to *class*. Indeed, in areas manifesting the cultural tone set by Protestant-

ism, the substantiality of status that arose with the division of labor
is likely to be expressed pragmatically, in terms of work. But
Protestantism's doctrine of the divinity in secular toil had fused
secular and supernatural "mystery" quite as Catholicism's divine
sanction for status had done. Hence, in either scheme, there was the
convertibility between the two kinds of "reverence," the social and
the religious. Consider, thus, Kafka's reference to the interchange-
ability of "vocation" and "life." He is talking of the way in which
Klamm (who represents the mystery of the courtly principle)
pervades K.'s sexual relations with Frieda. And he is saying in effect
that here the social motives of status ("vocation") become so
interwoven with universal motives ("life") that they can exchange
places. Recalling the nature of the book, in which the Castle
fluctuantly represents both the superiority of social caste and the
superiority of the godly, do we not see in this passing remark a
grotesque way of fusing both kinds of "reverence" (the social and the
"divine") in terms of sexual relations?

Since the religious motivation in Kafka is explicitly recognized
by both such authorities as Thomas Mann and Kafka's friend Max
Brod, we shall not pause here to establish it. But perhaps the single
sentence that most quickly conveys this quality is in the second
paragraph of the eighth chapter:

> When K. looked at the Castle, often it seemed to him as if
> he were observing someone who sat there quietly gazing
> in front of him, not lost in thought and so oblivious of
> everything, but free and untroubled, as if he were alone
> with nobody to observe him, and yet must notice that he
> was observed, and all the same remained with his calm not
> even slightly disturbed; and really—one did not know
> whether it was cause or effect—the gaze of the observer
> could not remain concentrated there, but slid away.

And in chapter 9, the discussion of things done "in the name of
Klamm," of things "filled by his spirit," or of a person who is but
"an instrument in the hand of Klamm," adds a transcendent dimension to the purely bureaucratic mystery. Images of storm and eagle
figure here too. Indeed, there is no trouble isolating the traditional
theological motive in this work. The problem, rather, as both the
Mann and Brod statements in the English translation indicate, is to

keep one reminded of the important role played here by the motives of social class.

What of the other two major themes of *The Courtier:* laughter and education (the themes gorgeously, almost hysterically, brought together in the Rabelaisian rhetoric)? In *The Castle,* the social rhetoric of laughter and education (two forms of "pure persuasion" this side of the religious) is not a subject of discussion, but is rather the essence of the work itself. The laughter, in its grotesque modification, is embedded in the very conception and method of the book, the oddly "humorous" treatment of reverence. The social bid in such expression is perhaps best revealed today in the mixture of grotesqueness and humor that distinguishes the "smartness" of the *New Yorker* sort (the "hierarchic" appeal of which is indicated in turn by the commercial advertisements that accompany it, advertisements obviously addressed to suburban, middle-class "elegance").

At one point, K. is told that the messenger Barnabas had cried when receiving his first commission. As a comment on the mystery, this incident is exceptionally telling. For Barnabas's first commission had been to communicate with K. And previously we had seen the mystery of Barnabas, as he looked to K. This sudden glimpse around the corner, with A mysterious to B and B mysterious to A, all because of their different participation in the mystery of C, does not merely dispel the illusion. For everyone goes on acting *as though* there were a mystery; and since acts are images, the mystery continues to be strong in our imagination. Indeed, once you learn the rules, once you are at home in its grotesque laughter, the very lack of motives for the mystery adds to the sense of mystery.

In a broken, grotesque version of courtship, we are not required to find counterparts for each of the elements in the symmetrical, classical version. Yet there do happen to be analogies for the educational principle. Judged as imagery, K.'s very role as land-surveyor, or rather, his attempt to get himself formally accredited in this role, involves the principle of education. For interpreted symbolically, a land-surveyor is surely one who would specify positions and elevations. And since this half-admitted, half-rejected K. so clearly represents the author, whose account of K.'s quandaries in confronting social hierarchy is itself a precise novelization of the hierarchic motive, it would hardly be exorbitant to say that Kafka here writes as a Jewish "intellectual." (He is "in" to the extent that an intellectual spontaneously considers himself superior to manual workers, as with K.'s attitude towards the peasants and workers of the village; he is "out" to the extent that an unnamed and even unnamable curse is upon him, a curse that keeps him permanently "guilty.") Kafka was "in" insofar as the intellectual spontaneously considers his status superior to that of the laboring classes, though he may "pastorally" court them, a social relation which a Leftist wag (he has since broken with the Party) formulated with suggestive gallantry, thus: "The intelligentsia must penetrate the proletariat." Kafka was "out" insofar as the intellectual class itself is somewhat suspect (though we will say for the Church, Aquinas's angels were pure intellectuals), and because in addition Kafka was Jewish in what was then preparing itself to become a part of Hitler's *Reich.*

Also, there is at least the image of education in the fact that, during much of his uncertainty, K. lives with Frieda in a school where he is supposed to be janitor, and where expressionistically the classroom he uses as living quarters is overrun by the schoolchildren. But the interweaving of education with the theme of childhood involves factors that belong rather under "grammar" and "symbolic." We have elsewhere noted the grammatical resources that permit logical priority to be stated narratively in terms of temporal priority. By such convertibility, the essence of the hierarchic principle (the Castle) can be identified with the conditions of childhood, since an esence is a logical "first," and childhood is a narrative first. Thus, near the beginning of the story, we are told that, at the first sight of the castle, "K. had a fleeting recollection" of the town in which he was born. The peasants are described as children, likewise the childish element in his assistants is commented on several times. When K. tries to phone the Castle, the receiver gives out a buzz that "was like the hum of countless children's voices—but yet not a hum, the echo rather of voices singing at an infinite distance." In the schoolroom where he lives with Frieda, their constant invasion of his privacy sets the mark of childhood upon the entire situation.

Again, the German word for castle, *Schloss,* has connotations of internality not present in the English equivalent. For it clearly suggests the idea of enclosure, being related to the verb for closing or locking, *schliessen. Klamm,* an adjective, means tight or close, related to another word for the act of enclosing, *klemmen.* We might recall the *hortus conclusus* of medieval thought, the ideal "closed garden" that duplicated the protectiveness of the walled town. And in the offing are the words for "advertising" and "calamity," *Reklam, Kalamität.*

So much for the grammar of "regression." From the standpoint of "Symbolic" note also that the imagery of childish sexuality is well suited to express the mystery of social courtship in one important respect: since social intercourse is not essentially sexual at all, such courtship is more nearly analogous to the "polymorphous-perverse" nature of infantile sexuality than to mature sexual mating. (See Shirley Jackson's novel, *The Road through the Wall,* for a subtle and sensitive representation of the ways whereby the unspeakable mysteries of social discrimination become interwoven, in childhood, with the unspeakable mysteries of the sexually unclean.) Since K.'s union with Frieda is but a roundabout approach to Klamm (who represents the mystery of the order headed in the Castle), there is a grotesque appropriateness in the fact that K. and Frieda are under the observation of others, even in the most intimate moments of lovemaking. Here are perhaps the strongest suggestions of the infantile, since children's experiments with sex lack intimacy, privacy, and purpose, quite as with the casual and almost absent-minded sexuality of Frieda and K.

The two major themes that complicate the analysis of *The Castle* in terms of grotesque courtliness are Kafka's illness and his personal conflicts with his father. Recalling Freud's suggestion that children are often figured in dreams as insects, we should probably find the clearest representation of the mysterious, troubled communication between father and son as different "kinds of being" expressed most directly in the story *The Metamorphosis,* about a son who was a monster cockroach. Rhetorically, we may note that, in this very disgrace of the offspring, there is a desperate vengeance against the parent from which it was descended.

Though the references to weariness in *The Castle* show signs of the author's personal illness, it is perhaps figured most clearly in the story of the *Hunger-Artist,* where the wastage of consumption has its analogue in the fantastic account of the performer who starved by profession. Anyone with a feeling for the grotesque might have hit upon the plot of this story as a conceit; but unless a writer were almost prodigiously imaginative, only by actually experiencing tuberculosis could he have developed this fictive counterpart of it with such gruesome thoroughness.

The disease here is also esthetically redeemed, as with much of Mann's work (*Tristan,* for instance) in becoming interwoven with the theme of art. (For a discussion of the story from this point of view, see R. W. Stallman's essay, "Kafka's Cage," in the Winter 1948 *Accent.*) There are rhetorical implications here, since the problem of being socially received is again considered, with much poignancy. And the rhetorical element that can arise even out of purely physical discomfitures is discernible in the identifications surrounding disease itself, as when Kafka writes: "Illness and weariness give even peasants a look of refinement." Thus such obsessiveness as comes of the Castle fits well with the imagery of disease, both physical and mental (or with such literary attenuations of mental disease as reside in the grotesque). For grammatically, disease is "passion," and as such can be a romantic and social analogue of the religious passion.

Kafka's study of law leads directly into rhetorical motives. The paper work, and the strongly hierarchic nature of legal administration could provide much material for the imagery of officialdom that is the basis of the courtliness. And behind positive law there always loom the questions of theologic law, as the castle looms above the village.

In his remarks on Kafka, Max Brod writes:

> The connection between the "Castle"—that is Divine Guidance—and the women, this connection half-discovered and half-suspected by K., may appear obscure, and even inexplicable, in the Sortini episode where the official (Heaven) requires the girl to do something obviously immoral and obscene; and here a reference to Kierkegaard's *Fear and Trembling* may be of value—a work which Kafka loved much, read often, and profoundly commented on in many letters. The Sortini episode is literally a parallel to Kierkegaard's book, which starts from the fact that God required of Abraham what was really a crime, the sacrifice of his child; and which uses this paradox to establish triumphantly the conclusion that the categories of morality and religion are by no means identical. The incommensurability of earthy and religious aims; this takes one right into the heart of Kafka's novel.

We might distinguish two important elements in this statement: the problem of the sacrifice (involving the interpretation of a story in Genesis 22) and the problem of the absurd (involving a doctrine of "incommensurability" between religious and social motives). They are so closely interwoven that we cannot discuss one intelligibly without implicating the other. Yet they might be separated for systematic purposes, since a cult of irrationality, or "the absurd," can be derived from many other sources than this chapter in Genesis, and a theory of sacrifice need not lay such stress upon the "kill" as marks Kierkegaard's interpretation of the biblical story.

The Undiscover'd Country:
The Death Motif in Kafka's *Castle*

W. G. Sebald

> *And in the end, or almost, to be abroad alone, by unknown ways, in the gathering of the night, with a stick. It was a stout stick, he used it to thrust himself onward, or as a defence, when the time came, against dogs and marauders. Yes, night was gathering, but the man was innocent, greatly innocent, he had nothing to fear, though he went in fear, he had nothing to fear, there was nothing they could do to him, or very little.*
>
> S. BECKETT, *Molloy*

The smooth surface of Kafka's work has remained an enigma in spite of what his interpreters have managed to dredge from its depths. It has preserved its integrity against the advances of criticism. What it conveys is the infinitely sombre gaze of the five-year-old boy who, dressed in a sailor suit and with a shiny black walking stick and a straw hat in his hand, was dragged into the gloomy exoticism of a photographer's studio in Prague. Critics have singularly failed to come to terms with this gaze, they have overlooked the yearning, fearful images of death which pervade Kafka's work and which impart that melancholy whose outset was as early as it was persistent. Sickness unto death, unless purged by suicide, has always been suspect in the eyes of society. It is therefore ignored, and instead one strives to wrest some positive meaning from Kafka's work—if necessary, in the spirit of the existentialist *volte face* whereby freedom emerges from the very absurdity of an endeavour. Such interpretations have been attempted in defiance of the obvious fact that Kafka

From *Journal of European Studies* 2, no. 1 (March 1972). © 1972 by Science History Publications Ltd. All translations of *Das Schloss* are taken from the Penguin edition.

felt constrained to hide any happiness he may have experienced like a physical deformity. It would mean a form of absolution for society if one could place a positive interpretation on K.'s desire for death, since it was society that instilled this grim, deep-seated desire in him in the first place and death—at least according to common superstition—is only a cipher for salvation.

Towards the end of the story K. converses with the landlady of the Herrenhof. " 'Didn't you once learn tailoring?' the landlady asked. 'No, never,' K. said. 'What actually is it you are?' 'Land Surveyor.' 'What *is* that?' K. explained, the explanation made her yawn. 'You're not telling the truth. Why won't you tell the truth?' 'You don't tell the truth either.' " He is not a surveyor then, he does not have anything with him to substantiate his claim, he is merely a wanderer, a figure who first appears with a "minute rucksack" and a "knotty stick." Psychoanalysis designates the image of a journey or a hike as a symbol of death, and Adorno [in *Moments Musicaux*] describes the scenario of Schubert's two great song cycles as follows: "They link up with poems in which again and again the images of death present themselves to the man who wanders among them as diminutively as Schubert in the Dreimäderlhaus. A stream, a mill and a dark desolate wintry landscape stretching away in the twilight of mock suns, timeless, as in a dream—these are the hallmarks of the setting of Schubert's songs, with dried flowers for their mournful ornament." Brown Bohemian earth, where at the end of the Middle Ages another German poet had once talked with death, also surrounds the Castle, as the pictures edited by Klaus Wagenbach show, and Kafka deliberately avoided introducing the brighter green of organic nature into his landscape as a source of comfort. The ground is covered in frost and snow, a still-life, a *nature morte* which precludes any hope of regeneration; this is reinforced by Pepi's statement that winter is long in these parts, so prolonged that in her recollection spring and summer appear to last barely more than two days, "and even on those days, even during the most beautiful day, even then sometimes snow falls." K. complains often enough that it is difficult to make any progress across this landscape. Aggravated by the monotony, the wanderer who tries to cross it always retraces his own tracks. "The eccentric structure of this landscape, where each point is equidistant from the centre, is revealed to the wanderer who traverses it without making any headway: every development is its own perfect antithesis, the first step is as close to death as the last, and the dissociated points of the landscape are visited in a circle, without it ever being left behind. For Schubert's themes wander just like the miller or the lover abandoned in winter by his mistress. They have no history but are merely viewed from different angles. The only change is a change of light." There can seldom have been a more apposite description of the way in which the avowedly unmusical Kafka circles about the geometric location of his yearning than in these lines of Adorno's on the structure of Schubert's work. The debate about K.'s "development" suddenly seems egregious, for at the point where in the first section of the book he crosses the wooden bridge over the stream and invades the territory of the Castle, he is like "those wretched souls who travel hither and thither but have no history" [as Walter Benjamin says]. The busyness in the *paysage mort,* all the to-ing and fro-ing of coaches and litigants, and every attempt to attain some goal in the domain of death bear the marks of immense futility. So too folklore tells us that in that undiscover'd country one takes three steps forward and three steps back. In the Berliner Ensemble production of *Mother Courage* the heroine marched against a revolving stage through the devastated lands of the Empire with no hope of ever changing her situation. K. too, the first time he tries to press on into the Castle, experiences a paralysis of the will to proceed imposed by some external force. "At last he tore himself away from the obsession of the street and escaped into a small side-lane, where the snow was still deeper and the exertion of lifting one's feet clear was fatiguing; he broke into a sweat, suddenly came to a stop, and could not go on." Kierkegaard describes the humorous equivalent of a progression directed against its own teleology in a passage devoted to the old Friedrichstädter Theatre in Berlin and a comedian called Beckmann.

> He can not only go, he can come and go at the same time. That's something quite different, to come and go simultaneously, and through this genial accomplishment he can improvise the whole physical setting and can not only represent a wandering journeyman but also come-and-go like one. We see it all, looking up from the dust of the highway towards a welcoming village and hearing its quiet sounds, glimpsing the very path which skirts the village pond where one turns off by the smithy—and there we see Beckmann approaching with his small haversack, his stick

in his hand, carefree and cheerful. He can come-and-go
followed by urchins whom one cannot in fact see.

(*Repetition*)

Adorno cites this passage in an essay on Chaplin. But Chaplin of
whom we are reminded by the adventures of Karl Rossmann and by
many photographs of Kafka himself—Chaplin who became hope-
lessly entangled in his own hastiness—was the hero of a modern
entertainment which Kafka described to Janouch as "the magic
lantern of a neglected youth," and all his life the neglect of youth
appeared to him like a premature death.

We learn only very little about the Castle itself, the imaginary
centre of the landscape of death. However, the figures that emerge
from it in the course of the story allow us to draw certain conclusions
about its nature. There is first of all Schwarzer who wakens the
weary K. from his unauthorized sleep. The name draws attention to
the colour that seems to be dominant in the Castle; its inhabitants,
like the assistants, wear close-fitting black clothes as a sort of
uniform. Yet the assistants themselves in spite of their sometimes
importunate liveliness, do not appear properly alive. When Artur
returns to the Castle in order to lodge a complaint about his master,
the latter realizes for the first time what he finds so repugnant about
Jeremias, the assistant who remains behind—it is "this flesh which
sometimes gave one the impression of not being properly alive."
And shortly afterwards the appearance of Jeremias confirms his
uncanny suspicion:

> As he stood there, his hair rumpled, his thin beard lank as
> if dripping with wet, his eyes painfully beseeching and
> wide with reproach, his sallow cheeks flushed, but yet
> flaccid, his naked legs trembling so violently with cold that
> the long fringes of the wrap quivered as well, he was like
> a patient who had escaped from hospital, and whose
> appearance could only suggest one thought, that of getting
> him back in bed again.

The tousled hair, the soaking beard, the eyes held open only with
difficulty, the loose flesh—it is as if Jeremias were already in a state
of decomposition, a corpse escaped from the grave. After all, "bed"
and "sleep" often stand for the abode and condition of the dead, in
this and other literature. When Frieda lets K. peep through the

spy-hole into Klamm's room, the latter is sitting completely immobile at his table. The only sign of life is a cigar smoking in his motionless hand and the glint of the pince-nez which hides his eyes—the most vital part of a man. Immediately afterwards K. wonders if Klamm is disturbed by the rowdiness of the servants. " 'No,' said Frieda, 'he's asleep.' 'Asleep?' cried K. 'But when I peeped in he was awake and sitting at the desk.' 'He always sits like that,' said Frieda, 'he was sleeping when you saw him. Would I have let you look in if he hadn't been asleep? That's how he sleeps, the gentlemen do sleep a great deal.' " Sleep is the brother of death and is assiduously cultivated by the inhabitants of the Castle. When they leave their bureaux to attend a hearing, they prefer to do it at night and even then they like to settle themselves in bed like Bürgel, that image of a regressive existence to which K. so fervently longs to return. Bürgel spends a large part of his time in bed, he deals with his correspondence in bed and interrogates plaintiffs from his bed. Unlike other officials Bürgel is plagued by insomnia. K. too is a restless spirit. This may be why Bürgel is willing and able to indicate a way out for K. Yet K., overcome by irresistible weariness, forfeits the chance of revelation, like the character in a Yiddish story who sleeps through the Day of Judgement. Sortini too, whom K. encounters only through Olga's story, is a harbinger of death. He is not one of those officials bloated with age, like Klamm, or one of those with child-like faces, like Bürgel: his features are rather different. Olga describes him as a small, weak, thoughtful person, and goes on, "and one thing about him struck all the people who noticed him at all, the way his forehead was furrowed; all the furrows—and there were plenty of them although he's certainly not more than forty—were spread fanwise over his forehead, running towards the root of his nose. I've never seen anything like it." A physiognomy such as Olga describes here reminds one readily of a mummy distorted by a shrinking process. However, it is not only this which makes the haggard Sortini an envoy of death, but also the scene where with legs stiffened by his sedentary occupation he leaps across the shaft of the fire engine to approach Amalia who is decked out like a bride. Politzer recognizes the fire service party where Sortini meets Amalia as a *sacre du printemps* but he omits to point out the affinity between the archetype of this ritual and that of death, even though the death symbolism surrounding the sacrificial feast of the maidservants can be shown to be a literary *topos*. Adrian

Leverkühn, for instance, is oppressed at the wedding of his sister by the fact that "the white shroud of virginity, the satin slippers of the dead" are used. Amalia is prepared for the firemen's festival in precisely the same manner. The "dress was specially fine," Olga recalls, "a white blouse foaming high in front with one row of lace after the other, our mother had taken every bit of her lace for it." Olga then describes the necklace of Bohemian garnets and reports her father as saying, "To-day, mark my words, Amalia will find a husband." But Amalia rejects Sortini's advances, is alarmed by the ghastly character of the spring rites and the absence of any conciliatory aspect which she may have hoped for in her more obscure presentiments. There are no tokens of any luxuriant scenery promising carefree procreation; of the requisites of the vernal season we glimpse only the bare date, July 3; and the centrepiece of the feast is a mechanical monster in the shape of the fire engine. For this reason Amalia refuses the next day to obey Sortini's summons which reaches her, according to Olga, in the form of a pornographic document drafted in copper-plate handwriting. For this reason too she brings down execration upon her family. Henceforth her father trudges each day up to the Castle entrance or to that of the cemetery, in order to draw the inhabitant's attention to himself and the sad lot of his family as they drive past in their carriages.

> In his best suit, which soon becomes his only suit, off he goes every morning from the house with our best wishes. He takes with him a small Fire Brigade badge, which he has really no business to keep, to stick in his coat once he's out of the village. . . . Not far from the Castle entrance there's a market garden, belonging to a man called Bertuch who sells vegetables to the Castle, and there on the narrow stone ledge at the foot of the garden fence father took up his post.

The best suit, soon to be the only one he will have left, the blessing of his family, the small medal, the market garden, the name of the gardener and the narrow stone ledge, all this recalls—if one translates the surreal fantasy images back into rational concepts—funerals and grave yards. The fact that shortly afterwards his wife follows the father on his excursions again adds to this picture of the death of the old couple. When Olga reports, "We often went out to them, to take them food, or merely to visit them, or to try to persuade them to come back home" here too the empirical equivalent is a visit to the cemetery and the graveside, the leaving of food for the wandering souls, still perpetuated in the sprinkling of holy water. Indeed the attempt to persuade the departed to return home is an archaic residue which had a great impact on Döblin when during a journey to Poland he visited the Jewish cemetery in Warsaw on the eve of the Day of Atonement. At home, however, the parents have left behind their stiff and helpless bodies which Amalia dresses and undresses, puts to bed and feeds, very much like Nag and Nell in *Endgame*.

When K. tries to reach the Castle, as he twice does at the beginning of his stay in the village, images of home well up involuntarily in his mind's eye. On the occasion of his first attempt, which ends with the regeneration scene in Lasemann's house, he is struck by the similarity between the Castle and the small town where he grew up, and he wonders whether it would not have been better to return home again instead of pressing on towards the Castle. The second time he believes himself to be approaching the Castle arm in arm with Barnabas, again a memory of home is conjured up.

> They went on, but K. did not know whither, he could discern nothing, not even whether they had already passed the church or not. The effort which it cost him merely to keep going made him lose control of his thoughts. Instead of remaining fixed on their goal they strayed. Memories of his home kept recurring and filled his mind. There, too, a church stood in the marketplace, partly surrounded by an old graveyard which was again surrounded by a high wall. Very few boys had managed to climb that wall, and for some time K., too, had failed. It was not curiosity which had urged them on. The graveyard had been no mystery to them. They had often entered it through a small wicket-gate, it was only the smooth high wall that they had wanted to conquer. But one morning—the empty, quiet marketplace had been flooded with sunshine, when had K. ever seen it like that either before or since?—he had succeeded in climbing it with astonishing ease; at a place where he had already slipped down many a time he had clambered with a small flag between his teeth right to the top at the first attempt. Stones were still rattling down under his feet, but he was at the top. He stuck the flag in,

it flew in the wind, he looked down and round about him,
over his shoulder, too, at the crosses mouldering in the
ground, nobody was greater than he at that place and that
moment.

Just as death has always been considered the second home of
mankind, so images of his first home flit through K.'s imagination
on his way to the Castle. Moreover Adorno [in *Minima Moralia*]
reminds us that Schubert too, "in the cycle revolving around the
words 'All my dreams are ended,' uses the name of 'inn' only for the
graveyard." The precise significance of such a notion can be seen
from K.'s clear memory of climbing the wall. What a crude
psychology is so quick to interpret as an unambiguous orgastic
symbol, in view of the ramming home of the flag and its taut
fabric—a symbol that conveys the conquering of death by the power
of life—is in fact anything but unambiguous even in K.'s mind. On
the contrary, the brief moment of triumph when to the boy looking
over his shoulder the crosses seem to sink into the ground is treated
as the expression of a short-lived surrender to personal happiness.
The cemetery exists just as before and then the teacher, a representative of realism, arrives and with a mere glance brings down the
whole house of cards. A more appropriate tool to help us understand
this episode and the context in which it appears would be Freud's
theory, developed in his later years, of the identity of the life and the
death wish. Freud regarded both as conservative, inasmuch as both
were concerned to escape from a state of spiritual and physical
individuation and to enter that condition of painlessness which is
beyond the birth trauma. Kafka considers this combination to be at
once comforting and hopeless in those passages where K. and Frieda
try to lose themselves in one another. We should not, of course,
overlook the significant but remote moment when, shortly after his
arrival, K. experienced in Frieda's arms the joy of a timeless
alienation from himself; yet this mirror of salvation is shattered by
the description not long afterwards of their futile endeavour to
recreate this *unitas unitatis*.

> There they lay, but not in the forgetfulness of the previous
> night. She was seeking and he was seeking, they raged and
> contorted their faces and bored their heads into each
> other's bosoms in the urgency of seeking something, and
> their embraces and their tossing limbs did not avail to

make them forget, but only reminded them of what they sought; like dogs desperately tearing up the ground they tore at each other's bodies, and often, helplessly baffled, in a final effort to attain happiness they nuzzled and tongued each other's face. Sheer weariness stilled them at last and brought them gratitude to each other. Then the maids came in. "Look how they are lying there," said one, and sympathetically cast a coverlet over them.

As so often with Kafka, a single isolated gesture at the end of a description seems to sum up its whole meaning. A sheet is spread over the twisted bodies who have died in love. It is well known that all the women characters in Kafka's novels remain tied to a stage of evolution that preceded the emergence of human life. There is, for example, the bloated Brunelda in *Amerika,* or Fräulein Bürstner, or Leni who has a bind of web between the middle and the fourth finger of her right hand as a token of her origins in some prehistoric swamp; and Frieda too, described as an etiolated creature who shuns the light, belongs to this group, as does Pepi who has risen from the chthonic depths of the Brückenhof, and Gardena, vegetating in her bed like a carnivorous plant. Walter Benjamin saw early on [in *Angelus Novus*] that these creatures belonged to a stage "which Bachofen calls the hetaeric." Its manifestation is that of self-forgetful life, and thus also of death. Just as the rotational correspondences of "hetaera esmeralda" haunt the compositions of Adrian Leverkühn after his exposure to the sting of death in the prostitute's embrace, so too Kafka's novels are permeated by the sombreness of a world where the dark forces of matriarchal figures unsex their male partners. These matriarchal figures, however, stand at the gates of Hell, for as Berthold von Regensburg tells us Hell lies at the heart of earth's steamy swamps. Such is the terrible ambivalence which cripples the power of life in Kafka's work. The death wish of love has its pendant in the message which K. believes he hears in the tolling of a bell, when Gerstäcker drives him back to the Brückenhof on his sleigh after the first fruitless expedition. "The Castle above them, which K. had hoped to reach that very day, was already beginning to grow dark, and retreated again into the distance. But as if to give him a parting sign till their next encounter a bell began to ring merrily up there, a bell which for at least a second made his heart palpitate for its tone was menacing, too, as if it threatened him with the fulfilment of his vague desire." As the promise is transformed into a threat of death, the tolling soon dies away, to be replaced by a less ambiguous sound, "by a feeble monotonous little tinkle which . . . certainly harmonized better with the slow-going journey, with the wretched-looking yet inexorable driver."

In the context of this argument, it would seem appropriate to explore the messianic traits which Kafka, more modest but also more serious than any of his contemporaries, bestows on his alter ego K. The limits of his messianic vision correspond to the great scepticism with which Kafka regarded the possibility of transcending the human predicament. Admittedly, since K. refuses to disclose to the village secretary Momus details of his identity and thus evades the regular admittance procedure into the realm of the dead, it could be argued he intends to invade the Castle as a living person and annul death's anathema on life. But all the other messianic hopes are imputed to him by others rather than being his own pretensions, and are therefore an example of those projections held to be the basis of human religion. K. initially represents a hope of this kind for Barnabas's family, a hope which even Olga fears towards the end of her tale is perhaps only an "illusion," for this family has always awaited the day when "someone in the long procession of visitors would arrive and put a stop to it all and make everything swing the other way again." But to bring the process to a halt, to dissipate the mythic power that reproduces itself in an eternal recurrence by forcing it to reverse its direction—this does not lie in K.'s power any more than in that of the young observer in Kafka's story *In the Gallery*. Like him, K. is dazzled and disoriented by the surface events, is himself drawn into the spectacle and thereby becomes guilty of complicity. "Then," Olga says, "we should have lost you, and I confess that you now mean almost more to me than Barnabas's service in the Castle." For Pepi too, the maid who lives in a damp celler, K. represents the epiphany of a better life. "At that time," we read, "she had loved K. as she had never loved anyone before; month after month she had been down there in her tiny dark room, prepared to spend years there, or, if the worst came to the worst, to spend her whole life there, ignored by everyone, and now suddenly K. had appeared, a hero, a rescuer of maidens in distress, and had opened up the way upstairs for her." The outcome of these hopes is familiar. After a short respite behind the bar Pepi has to return to the world from which she came, and it looks as if K. goes with her, after losing Frieda and his job as a caretaker. The saviour cannot come up to the great expectations held of him and sinks to the level of those who on his arrival looked up to him in hope. In this connection the episode with Hans Brunswick takes on a curious ambivalence. K. mentions to him that at home he used to be called " 'The Bitter Herb' on account of his healing powers." The "bitter herb" can stand for gentle hippocratic healing or be a symbol of death. The doctor is a secularized messiah who expels sickness from the suffering body but he is also the accomplice of death. This ambiguity, present at an early stage in Kafka's work, can be seen in the child's attitude to the stranger. The optimistic energy of the child—for "nobody is more eager to change things than a child" [as Kafka says elsewhere]—tries to overcome K.'s ambivalence, and out of the contradiction there arises in him:

> the belief that though for the moment K. was wretched and looked down on, yet in an almost unimaginable and distant future he would excel everybody. And it was just this absurdly distant future and the glorious developments which were to lead up to it that attracted Hans; that was why he was willing to accept K. even in his present state. The peculiar childish-grown-up acuteness of this wish consisted in the fact that Hans looks on K. as on a younger brother whose future would reach further than his own, the future of a very little boy.

Hans's desires, themselves conditional, do not inspire K. to any messianic gesture; rather they arouse "new hopes in him, improbable, he admitted, completely groundless even, but all the same not to be put out of his mind." Thus all hope remains circular and in the end it is no more than a "misunderstanding," as Bruno Schulz, Kafka's Polish translator, put it. Yet the messianic ideal is imputed to K. once again. Towards the end of the novel he finds himself by mistake in Bürgel's room on his way to an interrogation and there falls into a heavy sleep while the secretary imparts to him vital information that will lead him out of his dilemma. As though under some kind of compulsion Bürgel explains to the sleeping K. the threat which at that very moment he poses to the totality of the system. "It is a situation," Bürgel elaborates, "in which it very soon becomes impossible to refuse to do a favour. To put it precisely, one is desperate; to put it still more precisely, one is very happy.

Desperate, for the defenceless position in which one sits here waiting for the applicant to utter his plea and knowing that once it is uttered one must grant it, even if, at least in so far as one has oneself a general view of the situation, it positively tears the official organization to shreds: this is, the worst thing that can happen to one in the fulfilment of one's duties." This is the promise of apocalyptic destruction, but the potential messiah has fallen asleep from weariness—in other words, has succumbed to the brother of death—and he does not hear the summons directed at him. At precisely the point when he draws closest to his own salvation and to the salvation he could offer to the rest of the world, he is also furthest away from it, because of the eccentric structure of Kafka's world. At precisely the moment when his spirit is called, K. is asleep. Bürgel's words which from the outset K. hears only as a distant murmur, fail to rouse him to a new life but rather lull him into a sleep from which there will not readily be an awakening. " 'Clatter, mill, clatter on and on,' he thought, 'you clatter just for me.' " In falling prey to the temptation of sleep and thus offending against Pascal's metaphysical commandment "Thou shalt sleep no more," K. averts the danger which an individual such as he represents for the Castle. Though this may be inevitable, it also conveys the crazy irony of all human endeavour to escape from the limitations of one's own existence. "One's physical energies last only to a certain limit"; explains a Mephistophelian Bürgel, "Who can help the fact that precisely this limit is significant in other ways too? No, nobody can help it. That is how the world itself corrects the deviations in its course and maintains the balance. This is indeed an excellent, time and again unimaginably excellent arrangement, even if in other respects dismal and cheerless." However, the latent messianic mission to invade the realm of the dead as a living saviour can be interpreted in another way, if one equates the realm of the dead with the place where one's forefathers are assembled. This search for a buried ancestral tradition is represented by one of those insignificant gestures which seem to offer a key to the Kafka enigma.

> The support of the arm above was no longer sufficient; involuntarily K. provided himself with new support by planting his right hand firmly against the quilt, whereby he accidentally took hold of Bürgel's foot, which happened to be sticking up under the quilt.

This surrealistic detail is a memory of orthodox Judaism, in which one sought to ensure a lasting contact with the departed by touching the feet of the corpse. Kafka has this gesture in mind at another point when he writes [in his *Diaries*]:

> In Hebrew my name is Amschel, like my mother's maternal grandfather, whom my mother, who was six years old when he died, can remember as a very pious and learned man with a long, white beard. She remembers how she had to take hold of the toes of the corpse and ask forgiveness for any offense she may have committed against her grandfather.

Klaus Wagenbach has moreover demonstrated the topographical similarity between Kafka's Castle and that of the village Wossek, from where his father's family originated. K.'s attempt to penetrate the rambling wings of this castle may then be interpreted as an effort to re-enter the spiritual traditions of his forefathers. Kafka often regretted how remote they seemed to him, alienated as he was by the process of assimilation. "I am as far as I know the most typical Western Jew among them," he writes in a letter to Milena, "this means, expressed with exaggeration, that not one calm second is granted me, nothing is granted me, everything has to be earned, not only the present and the future, but the past too—something after all which perhaps every human being has inherited, this too must be earned, it is perhaps the hardest work." Small wonder if at the conclusion of the novel (which cannot be too distant from the point where the extant fragment tapers off) K. would, according to Max Brod, have died of exhaustion; small wonder indeed if he has to pay with his life to achieve proximity with his ancestors.

There are other images of death in the landscape surrounding Kafka's Castle. Folklore teaches us that the inn is an ancient symbol of the underworld. It is the place where the dead assemble before descending into Hell, and in legend the devil's tavern is the last stage on the journey of the dead. Like the Brückenhof it stands on the border of the other world. Even the architecture of the Herrenhof has something of a subterranean atmosphere, above all when the servant leads K. across the yard and

> then into the entry and through the low, somewhat downward-sloping passage. . . . The servant put out his

lantern, for here it was brilliant with electric light. Every-thing was on a small scale, but elegantly finished. The space was utilized to the best advantage. The passage was just high enough for one to walk without bending one's head. Along both sides the doors almost touched each other. The walls did not quite reach to the ceiling, probably for reasons of ventilation, for here in the low cellar-like passage the tiny rooms could hardly have windows.

And then the noise is described, a chaos of sound, of dictating and conversing voices, the clink of glasses and the blows of a hammer—a cacophony which may well have appeared as the most appropriate image of Hell to a Kafka notoriously sensitive to noise. The fact that coaches are used for travelling about similarly fits into the landscape of death, as does the telephone, that mystagogic instrument to which Proust and Benjamin paid such eloquent tribute. It is from the telephone that K. hears the same eleusinian humming which many of us remember from childhood walks beside the telegraph wires and which made a peculiarly melancholy impression. But the clearest evidence that the administrative apparatus of the Castle is occupied with the endless cataloguing of the dead comes from the claim that despite all confusion and contradictions nobody can slip through the official net. What strikes us as the most disconsolate aspect of this sphere of death is the fact that even here, just as in life, the powerful and the helpless are separated, that (again in accordance with folk lore) the village people dwell together in one room beneath the earth, while the gentlemen occupy a castle as in their previous existence. Finally a particularly valid argument for K.'s proximity to death when he enters the village is proffered by Ronald Gray's book on *The Castle*. In his interpretation of the last scene of the novel fragment, Gray does not, admittedly, arrange the death symbols which he discusses into the kind of pattern described above; in his view K. encounters death here almost by accident: it appears as a reflection of a narrative convention rather than a long since anticipated event. The landlady of the Herrenhof talks in this passage about her strange old-fashioned and over-crowded wardrobe, about dresses reminis-cent of the *pompes funèbres* to whose dusty vulgarity K. has taken exception. "If the dresses," Gray writes, "are the disguises which the hostess is accustomed to wear when she announces to men the moment of their death, a good deal falls into place." The landlady as Mistress World, as a barmaid in an inn belonging to the Devil, occurs in a poem by Walter von der Vogelweide, and Rilke in his elegy dedicated to travelling acrobats pays homage to the very same allegorical persona as Kafka when he recalls the place "where the modiste Madame Lamort / winds and binds the restless ways of the world, / those endless ribbons, to ever-new / creations of bow, frill, flower, cockade and fruit, / all falsely coloured, to deck / the cheap winter-hats of Fate" (5th *Duino Elegy,* ll. 88–94). It is, then, safe to assume that Gray is correct in his interpretation of this last scene and after all that has been said, it is manifest that the Kafka fragment could scarcely have found a more precise ending; here the fragmentary character of the novel transcends itself. This ending is appositely summarized in Gray's commentary as follows:

> The Charon-like figure of Gerstäcker already has K. by the sleeve, to carry him away on his flat, seatless sledge. On the preceding page the hostess seemed to be giving him instructions about K.'s destination. And now the hostess concludes with the possibly ambiguous remark: "To-morrow I shall be getting a new dress; perhaps I shall send for you."

That K. has attained the end of his natural course can only be regarded as a source of comfort and salvation as one compares it with the alternative that might have befallen him: to remain an eternal "stranger and pilgrim" on earth, as in the legend of Ahasver, the Wandering Jew. And to avoid this fate, K. seeks out the land of death of his own accord, for as he says in rejecting Frieda's dream of emigrating to Spain or the South of France, "What could have enticed me to this desolate country except the wish to stay here?" The yearning for peace which in K.'s world only death itself can provide, and the fear of being unable to die (like the hero of Kafka's "Gracchus the Huntsman"), the fear of a perpetual habitation in the no-man's land between man and thing—that yearning, that fear must be reckoned the ultimate motive for K.'s journey to the village whose name we never learn. Yet this village is at once the place where Jean-Paul causes the souls who have reached it to sigh, "At last we are in the courtyard of eternity and but one more death and we shall see God."

The Castle: To Deny Whatever Is Affirmed

Ronald Gray

In September 1917, [Kafka's] tuberculosis was diagnosed. Kafka knew he had not long to live; he moved to the village of Zürau, to join his sister Ottla, and remained there till the following summer. Meanwhile his second engagement to Felice, made in July, was broken off in December 1917. Little was written during this extremely difficult time. Kafka was broken with grief, as Brod relates, after seeing Felice to the train for the last time: "His face was pale, hard, severe. But suddenly he began to weep. I shall never forget the scene, one of the most terrible I have ever witnessed. . . . Kafka had come straight to me in my office, at the busiest time of day, and sat next to my desk in the armchair that stood there for petitioners, pensioners, and people under prosecution. And here he wept, asking with sobs: 'Isn't it terrible that this sort of thing has to happen?' The tears were running down his cheeks. I have never seen him, except on this one occasion, distraught and without composure."

The decision had been a deliberate choice: it was either marriage or writing, although the same choice had to be faced later more than once, with other women. For a time, however, his creative writing did not benefit directly, though more philosophical work, especially aphorisms, was produced. It was not until 1920 that a flow came such as he had experienced in 1912, 1914 and 1917. Meanwhile, Zürau had possibly supplied an impetus to the novel he was to begin

---

From *Franz Kafka.* © 1973 by Cambridge University Press. All translations of *Das Schloss* are by Willa and Edwin Muir.

a few years later: certainly he spoke of a new novel, and the study of peasant-life in Zürau could well have contributed to some scenes in *The Castle,* though a tale begun in 1914 ("Temptation in the Village") had first embodied the general idea. (Other geographical possibilities, especially Wossek, a village about sixty miles south of Prague, are discussed by Wagenbach [in *Kafka-Symposion*].) By 1922, his life had altered considerably. Though still in theory employed at the insurance office, he had spent a great deal of time in sanatoria. He had also fallen deeply in love with a young Czech woman, the translator of some of his works, Milena Jesenská, with whom his relationship was easier than any he had known hitherto, perhaps just because she was both unhappily married and unwilling to leave her husband, so that Kafka and she saw little of each other and yet felt most tenderly. These were almost ideal circumstances, for a man placed as he was: here was a woman he could love, yet to whom he could not be married and who would thus not impede his writing. The new situation is reflected in *The Castle,* begun in January 1922, but abandoned, unfinished, in the autumn of the same year. For all that, the atmosphere of *The Castle* is often as oppressive as that in any of Kafka's works. Though the action moves from place to place within the village, the streets are always deserted, the rooms are cramped, there is frustration and confusion at almost every turn, the Castle itself looms over the houses yet is always inaccessibly remote. It seems to be always night, with snow falling, and the novel breaks off at a moment when K. appears about to be going to narrow quarters below ground rather than pressing on to his first goal, the most interior recesses of the Castle organisation. Yet out of this darkness and choas Kafka makes a novel with more moving humanity, greater strength and subtlety of writing, more complexity of structure, more comprehensive scope than any he had written so far. It remains, like *The Trial,* partly a dream-novel: there are scenes which have all the incongruities, the obsessive acceptance of improbabilities, that belong to dreams. But the conscious mind has had more control in the writing, and the movement of the imagination has been more steady than it was in the fragmentary *Trial.* There are no stoppings and startings in *The Castle,* characters do not appear only to disappear, but are interrelated from the first moment, and the threads of action are distinct from the first pages: the attempt to gain an interview with the supreme official Klamm, with its ramifications into interviews with lesser officials, Momus, Bürgel and Erlanger, interweaves with K.'s attachment to Klamm's mistress Frieda, and this in turn interweaves with Frieda's hostility to Amalia as the woman who has rejected the love of a Castle official. *The Trial* resembles *The Great Wall of China* in the isolation and incompleteness of its chapters. *The Castle,* like *The Metamorphosis,* shows by its chapter-divisions, each chapter being complete in itself, yet leading on to the next, how much on this occasion Kafka's conscious mind is active, while at the same time the subconscious flow, the absence of any predetermined purpose, leads the novel forward in a mysterious way that holds the reader's attention because he himself is as much involved in the bafflement as K. is, and looks in the same way for a solution.

The conscious mind within the dream shows up, in contrast to *The Trial,* in the greater determination K. now shows. It would not have been like Joseph K. to have answered, as K. does in *The Castle,* "That's enough of that nonsense," certainly not to have used words like those "surprisingly gently." It would have been equally unlike Joseph K. to have said, as K. does after the Superintendent has explained official procedures, "So the upshot is that it's all very unclear and insoluble except that they throw you out." That kind of directness is something new, and it fits with the general behaviour of K., which is active where Joseph K.'s is passive, critical where his is acquiescent, positive where his is negative. The contrast can be taken too far, but there is little doubt that in making K. come to the village and so to the Castle organisation, rather than letting it come to him, Kafka was deliberately reversing the situation of *The Trial.* The new K. is a man who would have at least attempted to pass the guard at the gate of the Law in the Court-chaplain's parable. Whether this amounts to a polarity, on a Hegelian model, as Emrich suggests, is a different matter. The reversal has been made, that much is true, but the conscious mind does not take over as it does, say, in the novels of Hermann Hesse, where dialectics play a schematic part. K. and Kafka remain largely ignorant or unknowing, the movement of the novel is not predetermined and can be sometimes painfully halting; that is the price that has to be paid. "It's true," K. says, "ignorant is what I am, that's a truth that remains, whatever you say, and it's sad for me; but there is the advantage that an ignorant man will dare more, and that is why I am willing to put up gladly with ignorance and its no doubt bad consequences at least for a short while, so long as strength lasts." Kafka does dare more, and the result is not only more stimulating, it is sometimes deeply moving. Nowhere else in Kafka's literary work, for one thing, is there any character who speaks as Frieda does, in the genuine accents of love:

> "If only," Frieda said, slowly, quietly, almost relaxedly, as if she knew she could have only a very short spell of peace resting on K.'s shoulder, but wanted to enjoy it to the full, "if only we had emigrated somewhere that first night, we could be in safety somewhere, always together, your hand always close enough to take hold of; how I need you near me, how desolate I have been, ever since I have known you, when you are not near; believe me, having you near me is the only dream I ever dream, no other."

More is at stake in *The Castle* than in *The Trial,* or rather there is more to be gained for K. Leaving aside for a moment what the Castle stands for, and why K. wants to enter it, it seems towards the end that if K. were to play his cards right he could "control everything" (not that that is ever his own stated ambition) whereas in *The Trial* his only prospect was at the very best acquittal, at worst execution. Again, whereas in *The Trial* the judges were represented as mean and vindictive men, trivially vain about their quite unimportant positions, yet never actually met with, K. both sees Klamm quite early in the story, and conceives of him before long as a being far superior to himself:

> The landlady had once compared Klamm to an eagle, and that had seemed ridiculous to K., but not now: he thought of his remoteness, his impregnable dwelling-place, his silences, broken perhaps only by cries such as K. had never heard, of his downward piercing gaze that could never be verified, never be refuted, of those circlings in the air that could never be destroyed from out of K.'s depths, and in which he wheeled about up there in accordance with incomprehensible laws, visible only for moments at a time: all that was in common between Klamm and the eagle.

Klamm is never represented as the judges are in *The Trial,* and although some aspects of the comparison with the eagle make him no more attractive than they—one notes too that K. seems to have some hope of destroying Klamm—this presentation of the adversary has a more stimulating effect than the wearisome accounts provided by Titorelli, not least in the vigour of the writing. Similarly the Castle, though K. never reaches it, is portrayed almost as a living being, seen before revealing itself, with qualities that it would be positively good to have:

> When K. looked at the castle it used to seem to him at times as though he were observing someone quietly sitting there gazing, not lost in thought and thereby shut off from everything, but free and untroubled, as though he were alone and observed by no one, but this did not disturb his quiet in the least. And sure enough—you couldn't tell whether as a cause or a consequence—an observer could not maintain his gaze, and let it slip aside.

These are definite statements about things seen, with meanings that can be ascertained, not vagueness piled on uncertainty, as the accounts of the invisible Court are, and the novel benefits from the change.

The Castle is altogether clearer, though the word is still relative to the clarity to be expected in Kafka. In choosing to write of a castle at all, Kafka may have thought to provide a general clue, though since some readers have found the theological interpretations "totally unsupported by internal evidence," the position needs to be spelled out a little. The notion of a castle as a spiritual goal is of some antiquity, and one need go no further than the work by Kafka's seventeeth-century fellow-countryman, Komensky (or Comenius), *The Labyrinth of the World and the Paradise of the Heart,* to find an analogy. It is true that Komensky's castle proves to be a false lure, though Kafka must certainly have thought of him at the town of Brandys, not far from Prague, where he is commemorated, and the mysticism of Komensky must have had some attraction for him. The only reference to him in Kafka's letters suggests, at the least, respect. Again, Kafka did not write a straightforward allegory in the sense of Komensky's pilgrimage or Bunyan's; his Castle remains mysterious even when some of the outlines have been seen. It may also be that Kafka was very slightly influenced by the realistic nineteenth-century Czech novel, *The Grandmother,* by Božena Němcová. But there is good reason for saying that Kafka's general drift is more easily understood in the terms which St Teresa of Avila used in her well-known work on the mystic's path to God:

> While I was beseeching our Lord today that he would
> speak through me . . . a thought occurred to me which I
> will now set down, in order to have some foundation on
> which to build. I began to think of the soul as if it were a
> castle made of a single diamond or of very clear crystal, in
> which there are many rooms, just as in Heaven there are
> many mansions.

In St Teresa's terms, the soul that reaches the innermost mansion of
her castle "is made one with God," but there is no need to suppose
that Kafka meant exactly the same as St Teresa. Unlike her, Kafka
gives no explanation, and some features of the Castle make it
impossible to reconcile with any Christian conception of God,
though people in the novel do speak of the Castle in the way that
people generally do speak of God. Still, there are sufficient similari-
ties for certain overtones to be unmistakably heard. In the long
passage on the inadequate telephone connections with the Castle
there is a play on the idea of prayer. It is largely ironical, unless it is
taken as showing prayer to be as apparently ineffective as it is often
said by mystics to be. There is also, however, a reference to sounds
heard in the village on the Castle telephone which suggests a more
important function. In the words of the Superintendent, there is no
trusting any verbal message that comes through from the Castle: on
the other hand there is a continual telephoning going on in the
Castle, which is heard in the village as humming and singing. This,
according to the Superintendent, is the only accurate and trustworthy
communication to be had, everything else is deceptive. And as he
says this, one cannot help being reminded (though Kafka's modern
setting gives a quite different tone) of Rilke's words from the *Duino
Elegies,* written at about the same time:

> Hearken, my heart, as only
> saints have done: till it seemed the gigantic call
> must lift them aloft. . . . Not that you would endure
> the voice of God—far from it. But heark to the suspiration,
> the uninterrupted news that grows out of silence.

The difference is that Kafka does not vouch for his message, as Rilke
seems to do: for Kafka it is merely one more feature of the Castle,
that this is said about it. But the implication he intends cannot be

ignored. Similarly, the role of Barnabas, K.'s appointed messenger to and from the Castle, seems to be that of an inefficient angel, and the long disquisition by the Superintendent on the infallibility of the Castle organisation, in chapter 5, has the same kind of obvious allegorical significance, with the same kind of ironical reserve, at least so far as Kafka is concerned. ("Are there inspectorates?" says the Superintendent. "There are nothing but inspectorates. Of course they are not there to detect errors in the crude sense of the word, because errors never occur, and even if an error were to occur, as in your own case, who is to say in the last analysis that it actually is an error." The satire on arguments about infallibility is obvious enough.)

Less obvious, but still striking as the pattern of the novel begins to unfold, is the curious hierarchy within the village, which seems to operate only among the women working in the two inns. It is a natural enough progression to move as Pepi does from chambermaid to barmaid, and it seems that a further step can be taken from there to the rank of landlady. But in the strange world of this novel these promotions seem to have spiritual or moral connections. When K. first meets Frieda, as a barmaid, he is struck by something in her eyes, a look of "remarkable superiority."

> When she happened to look at K., it seemed to him that there was something about her eyes that had already accomplished things that had to do with him, things he as yet did not so much as suspect, yet which must exist, the eyes convinced him of that.

The landlady at the Bridge Inn, however, is even more imposing, despite her fits of bad temper. When she first appears to K., he sees her knitting in a chair, a gigantic figure, "almost darkening the room," and there are many suggestions that she is a woman of great spiritual power. Much the same is true of Klamm, who is talked about by the landlady in terms that sound fantastic or melodramatic: she asks how K. could withstand the look in Klamm's eyes, and admits that she herself could not withstand it without a door in between, so that again one is reminded (though a note of irony is presumably present in Kafka) of Rilke's at that time still unpublished *Elegies,* and the Angels who are terrifying in their sheer presence:

>   And even if one of them suddenly
> pressed me against his heart, I should fade in the strength of his
> stronger existence. . . . Each single angel is terrible.

This is not to say that Klamm has anything angelic about him. In so far as the name suggests anything—and names do occasionally have significance in Kafka's work—it is a normal German word for a narrow ravine, and suggests the verb "klammern": to clutch, cling, or hang on. As an adjective it means numb, stiff with cold, or damp, and beginning with a *k* it may have vague suggestions of being appropriate to K.'s case. In short, it is ambiguous, partly suggesting an embrace (but a convulsive or desperate one), partly remoteness or constriction. Yet Klamm has extraordinary powers, as not only the landlady but also Frieda says: it is Frieda who believes that it was "Klamm's work" that brought her and K. together in the bar, and Frieda's view, according to the landlady, that "everything that has happened is the will of Klamm." These are hints obvious and irrefutable enough, though they are not obtrusive within the novel, coming rarely and in a setting where the impression of ordinariness predominates. Klamm, as K. actually sees him, is a fat, thick-set, slightly ageing man with a long black moustache and a pince-nez set awry on his nose, who sits with a glass of beer smoking a cigar. The physical description would suit well the photographs of Kafka's father, and Kafka certainly had an earthly father in his mind, though he cannot have expected his readers to know that. Yet the fact that he places the suggestive phrases in the mouths of the two women, not in K.'s own, implies that Kafka did not wish them to be thought of simply as K.'s or his own subjective and absurd magnifications of his father's importance.

But it is not Klamm that K. wants to meet, or rather Klamm is only a stage on the journey. Somewhere beyond, though only briefly mentioned, is the owner of the Castle, the oddly-named Count Westwest. (Heinz Politzer surmises that an intensified decline of the sun may be implied, but it is anybody's guess.) Is it the Count whom K. expects to meet? We are never actually told, and here one of the questionable elements in the novel begins to show itself: the reader is never told why K. wants to meet Klamm, whether he regards him as a final authority, or why he should think of destroying him. Part of K.'s purpose is clear—he wants confirmation of his appointment by the Castle as a surveyor, and in this a certain human indecision on the value of activity in general can be understood. K. has been summoned as a surveyor, or so he says, yet there is no knowledge of his appointment when he first arrives, and in this a quite usual doubt about the authenticity of one's vocation may be reflected. For Kafka it may well have been a doubt about his value as a writer (and "surveyor" is not a bad metaphor for "novelist"), strong though his conviction was that there was no other career open to him. Doubts about writing, at all events, are the gist of his story "Josephine the Singer," in which he presents an "artist" about whom there are considerable doubts whether her art deserves the name at all. In the same way, there are extreme doubts about whether or not K. is "called" to be a surveyor: the question is never remotely near to being solved from the beginning to end. That in itself, of course, is no criticism of the novel. It is some criticism, though, to say that from beginning to end K. shows no sign of ever having had any smattering of knowledge of surveying, never shows any wish to survey, or any hint of what surveying might be done. It may be, as Erich Heller once suggested, that the word "Landvermesser," "land-surveyor," is a pun involving the verb "sich vermessen," "to have false pretensions," but the hint could very properly have been developed, had Kafka wanted to do so. As it is, there is the bare statement that he is appointed as surveyor, and no clue whether he could carry out the work if he were asked to do so. He accepts the assistants appointed by the Castle although they confess that they themselves have no knowledge of the subject, and he apparently realises very well that they are not what they claim to be, not the assistants who he originally engaged. And thus an element of uncertainty is present that could quite simply have been removed, and which seems merely meant to mystify. Is K. a surveyor, has he any right to expect recognition at all? The fact that absolutely no clue is given makes it possible for endless speculation to go on, but it is speculation about nothing, rather like the priest's comments on his own parable in *The Trial,* and it is just this kind of speculation that gives rise to tedium. K.'s vocation is as groundless as Joseph K.'s guilt.

The mystery does seem to lift a little near the beginning of chapter 5, when K. reflects on the difference between himself and the officials. They, he observes, are defending distant and invisible things on behalf of distant and invisible masters, whereas K. was fighting for something living and close, for himself, and moreover, at least at the outset, by his own will, for he was the attacker; and not only he was fighting for himself, but evidently other powers also, which he knew nothing of, but in whom he could believe in view of the measures taken by the authorities.

That K. is fighting for his living ("meine Existenz," as he puts it—the overtones are more positively audible in the German) is intelligible. Yet here again, there is promise of more than is offered. What are the measures which lead him to believe that other powers are fighting for him (or for themselves; the German is not wholly unambiguous)? Again there is no clue, so that the writing begins to attract the suspicion of being merely mystifying, in a way that is really not impressive when the author seems either to be withholding information or to be putting down words which he is not concerned to back up. It is one thing to be "unknowing," and another not to let the reader know.

Part of Kafka's intention must certainly be to cast doubt on whether K.'s experience has anything more than a subjective validity. The Castle itself is explicitly said to be not a castle in the sense of a fortress or a chateau, but "an extensive construction consisting of a few double-storeyed buildings and a large number of lower buildings huddled together." If one had not known it was a castle, Kafka goes on, one might have thought it was a small town, and the important thing is that it corresponds to K.'s expectations. Just as, in *The Trial,* the Court-room is in a place which K. almost stumbles into by accident, and the Court reproves him for coming an hour later than he had privately intended, though no particular time had been appointed, so the Castle lives up to K.'s idea of what it is to be. Since he insists that he is the surveyor, the Castle agrees, and even sends him a letter telling him that, "as he knows," he has been appointed. Since he claims to have assistants, the Castle sends him two, and in accepting them K. seems to enter into the spirit of the game. All these incidents could imply that K.'s quest is solipsistic. The impressiveness of some of the allusive remarks about Klamm and the others loses some of its weight if that too was merely a reflection of K.'s expectations. He cannot be fighting for himself or for his existence if the opposition is no more than a mirage conjured up by his own wishes; there would be nothing to fight in that case.

Yet there is a good deal that does not simply correspond to what K. expects. K. is not an easily likable man, at any rate for the greater part of the novel: he can be surprisingly, even childishly vindictive at times, when he throws a snowball at Gerstäcker's ear in a fit of pique, or goes looking for his assistants with a willow-rod in his hand, swishing it against his side in gleeful expectation. He may be in love with Frieda, as she certainly is with him, but he never does her any loving service or kindness, and he has an arrogant way with people in general. On the other hand, the Castle organisation, in the early chapters at least, seems intent on showing itself at its most benevolent, and the villagers, with a few exceptions, are very willing to offer help and advice, even if it is not always what K. wants. It is not stretching things to say that Kafka seems to have reversed the situation of *The Trial* not only by making K. active not passive, but also by making the organisation confronting him more sympathetic. But in doing this, Kafka lets fall an observation that offers a valuable clue perhaps to the whole of his work. Having conceived of the Castle (at all events at this early stage of the novel) as a mainly benevolent institution, even though an unattainable one, Kafka writes of the moment when K. withdraws after his first attempt at reaching it:

> But as if to give him a sign of parting, for the time being, a bell began to ring gaily up there, a bell which at least for a moment made his heart leap, as if it were threatening him—for the sound was melancholy too—with the fulfilment of his uncertain desire.

Apart from the difficulty of imagining the sound itself, being both gay and painful or melancholy, this passage presents the reader with the revealing information that K.'s desire is not only uncertain, he would actually prefer not to realise it, not to have it fulfilled. The suggestion of a deliberate, perhaps systematic commitment to frustration ought not to pass without comment. It may help to explain some of the developments later in the novel.

For there are quite strong suggestions that the Castle is well disposed, and that in looking for help from the women in closest touch with it—the mistresses of Klamm, that is—K. is not going wrong as Josef K. was said to do in *The Trial,* where women were merely a hindrance. The picture of Frieda is quite different from that of Fräulein Bürstner: she is a warm-hearted, sympathetic woman with a ready kiss for K., a willingness to get on with household jobs and to sacrifice her own interests for his, which distinguish her totally from any other woman in Kafka's work. Her first encounter, when she tears so savagely and desperately at him, is out of keeping with the picture given of her later, and the expression "a mistress of Klamm's" ("Geliebte"—"Love" or "beloved") gains some honour from its connection with her. There may well be an autobiographical element here. Kafka wrote to Milena of his hesitation in putting so much hope as he did in another human being like herself, a hope which he spoke of even as blasphemous. Yet he also spoke in the same letter of something divine in her human face, and the bridge she provided for him, at least for a while, is reflected in several moving passages in *The Castle* about the relation between women and Castle officials. At times the relation suggests a mystical love. When the landlady at the Bridge Inn puts round her head the shawl which is one of her mementoes of Klamm, she lies quite peacefully, and all suffering seems to be lifted from her. The love she felt, as K. sees it, was a blessing which she was unable to draw down for her own and her husband's benefit, it was not in the least like the purely self-seeking love shown by Leni in *The Trial*. But it is not only the women who have been in love with Klamm who are impressive. Olga, who belongs to the family of Barnabas, ostracised because her sister Amalia refused to give in to an official, is more companionable than the landlady by far, she shows a peaceful happiness in being able to sit by the stove with K., no trace of jealousy visible: "and this very absence of jealousy and consequently of severity of any kind, did K. good. He was glad to look into these blue eyes, not tempting him, not ordering him about, but shyly resting, shyly holding their own." Barnabas himself has much the same gentleness, with a kind of humility in his smile which would be completely refreshing to K. if he were only better at delivering K.'s messages.

Yet the pattern of the novel can only have been intended to overturn the mainly benevolent picture built up in the early chapters. The first twelve chapters are comparatively full of incident—the arrival, the first attempt at reaching the Castle, the receipt of Klamm's letter, the settling-in with Frieda at the Bridge Inn, the attempt to waylay Klamm, give a movement to the novel which is not much halted by tedious speculations and explanations such as those of the mayor (or elder), who has too close a resemblance to Titorelli in this respect. By the twelfth chapter, it is true, some evidence of hostility to K. has begun to emerge, especially in the behaviour of Gisa the schoolmistress, and the schoolmaster. But it is not until chapter 15 that anything amounting to a possible indictment of the Castle is seen, and when this does come there is not only an element of contrivance, the writing becomes almost totally obsessive. It is in this chapter, of course, that Olga begins to relate the story of how Amalia was seen by the official Sortini (suggesting perhaps the Italian for "fate") and summoned to satisfy his lust, how Amalia refused, and how since that day the whole family has sunk into disrepute throughout the village. (Similarly, K. fears in *The Trial* that the accusation against him will ruin his family.) The purpose of this within the framework of the whole novel—or at any rate the function—is clear enough. The benevolence of Klamm, and the genuine attachment felt for him by Frieda and the landlady, with all that that implies, is to be shown as only one aspect of an ambiguous organisation, which occasionally treats village women with nothing but contempt. It is not impossible to see religious analogies here, if one wants to do so, for although Jehovah is shown mainly in a benevolently loving relation to women—for instance in Ezekiel 16—the relations of Zeus with women were often more analogous to Sortini's, and if Kafka's intention was to comment on the ambivalent feelings of some women in relation to the divine, he had ample opportunity here.

He may also have intended to introduce, as Brod suggests, a parallel with the situation analysed at such length in Kierkegaard's *Fear and Trembling,* that is, the "teleological suspension of the ethical" implied by God's command to Abraham to kill his son Isaac. In other words, where the divinity requires of men what normally seems to them iniquitous, it is the duty of a truly religious man to obey with a glad heart. But if that was part of Kafka's intention, the point is only obscurely dealt with, and nothing challenging either way is said.

Clearly, Kafka had the Sortini incident in mind from quite early on, since Frieda's animosity towards Amalia is shown at their very first meeting, and that animosity expresses the difference between a woman who has gladly accepted love from a Castle official, and one who has rejected it. The difficulty about the whole of this very long sequence, however, is not at all that an element of ambivalence and conflict is introduced. On the contrary, these could heighten the interest. It is rather that the doubts expressed are so total as to seem parodistic of doubt, and that the writing goes completely to pieces. Olga attempts—and here the contrivance shows all too clearly—to persuade K. that there is really no essential difference between the way that Frieda was treated and the way Amalia was, although it is quite clear that the insulting letter sent by Sortini to Amalia had no parallel in any letter from Klamm. The underlying purpose seems to be to show that nothing definite can be predicated of the Castle or its officials at all. "The letter to Amalia," Olga argues, "may have been thrown on to the paper in thoughts, completely regardless of what was really being written. What do we know about the thoughts of Castle gentlemen?" This kind of argument is of course very close once again to the style of the Court chaplain. If the words in the letter do not represent the thoughts of Sortini, there is no need to pay any attention to them, Amalia did not refuse any order of his, and the whole affair is blown up out of all proportion, however irresponsible Sortini was. But this is typical of Olga's way of talking in this chapter, and not insignificant for the novel as a whole. Olga goes on, not long after this, to express doubts of the same all–embracing kind, quite out of keeping with the earlier description of her serenity. It is not only that she again throws all notion of meaning arbitrarily to the winds, she speaks as nobody could who was "resting," and "holding her own." For Olga as she is now represented, the idea of a village-girl not loving a Castle official is unthinkable: all girls do, if opportunity offers:

> "But you object that Amalia did not love Sortini. Well, yes, she did not love him, but perhaps she did love him all the same, who can decide on that? Not even she herself. How can she imagine she did not love him when she rejected him more forcefully than any official, probably, has ever been rejected before."

This is either irritating the reader, who must object that people in love know very well whether they are in love or not, or it is making Olga share the absurd position of the Superintendent, in an earlier chapter, who seems to be offered merely as an object of irony. But if no one in his right senses could be impressed by the kind of argument about the impossibility of error put forward by him, what is it doing in the mouth of Olga, who to all appearances was a rational woman with a strong reserve of good sense? The most likely explanation is that Kafka himself, in obsessed moments, was prone to think in this way—there are passages of this kind often enough to justify the supposition, especially since they are not confined to one character or type of character, but distributed as though at random. Kafka's characters are scarcely ever distinguished by their habits of speech or processes of thought: all of them are capable of spinning on in the same indeterminate way, and though one or another may object more concretely from time to time, there is no consistency in the objections either: they are momentary flashes, not seriously weighed-up counterbalances. Olga, like the Superintendent, talks interminably for the reason that neither of them take words seriously. Words are for her often ciphers with no particular meaning, so that to say that a person is or is not in love is a matter of indifference.

This shows itself also in the writing, where a certain habitual tendency of Kafka's to use concessionary words shows itself here in the excessive use of "gewissermaßen" ("to a certain extent"), a word which he can scarcely have used often with a convinced sense of its appropriateness. One finds Olga saying that certain kinds of villagers are "to a certain extent extremely" appetising for Castle officials; one finds Bürgel saying that some opportunities are "to a certain extent too large" to be used, and the landlady saying that Klamm "to a certain extent did not at all" ("gewissermaßen gar nicht") summon Frieda to him a second time. These are uses which reveal the same kind of permanent and ungrounded indecision as Olga shows about Amalia's love. Yet this ungrounded and impossible indecision, the characteristic of neurotic hesitation, is the ground bass of page after page, especially after chapter 15 has begun, and the attempt is being made to show the benevolence of the Castle as essentially ambivalent. To have shown Klamm and Sortini existing side by side as representatives of the Castle would have been perfectly reasonable and not without allegorical point, from a religious point of view. In trying to make them appear indistinguishable, Kafka is obliged to abandon the rational use of words, which is as much as to say, to abandon words at times altogether.

This is the reason, too, for the increasing obsessive use of certain words as the novel goes on.

All his life, Kafka was prone to write in a ruminative but inconclusive way, and a small number of words increasingly force themselves on the attention. "Gewissermaßen" ("to a certain extent") with its retreat from definite assertion, is found surprisingly often even in early writings; its habitual use in *The Castle* has just been seen. "Perhaps" and "probably" come much more frequently, and there is a constant sense of possibilities being tentatively weighed up and just as tentatively either deprecated or approved: "indeed . . . yet" ("zwar . . . aber"), "for that matter" ("übrigens"), "naturally," or "it must be confessed" ("freilich"), "at all events" and several others recur with such frequency as to be uncomfortably noticeable. At times in the later writings, as in "The Burrow," or "Josephine the Singer," the whole structure of a story depends on such a flow of half-assertions, concessions, renewed assertions and renewed yieldings to contrary promptings, and at times these amount to no more than an inconsequential rambling. When Titorelli or Huld, in *The Trial,* confuse themselves in this way, it is understandable as the natural utterance of characters who have little notion of what they are talking about; it amounts to satire. There are comparatively few instances of such words in stories like "In the Penal Colony" and *The Metamorphosis.* In the later stories, and particularly in the later stages of *The Castle,* they occur so often and so improbably as to raise the question whether Kafka was always in a condition to direct them.

With time, literally nothing can be said without a concession to a possible different point of view, whether such a view is reasonable or not, and the concessions can increase to the point where Kafka does lose control:

> "So my plan had actually failed," says Olga, "and yet did not fail completely, for while indeed we did not find the messenger, and my father's continual journeys to the Herrenhof inn and staying the night there, and perhaps even his sympathy, so far as he is capable of that, unfortunately finished him off—he has been in the condition you saw him for two years now, and yet perhaps he is better off than my mother, whose death we expect every day, and which is only delayed by Amalia's excessive exertions. But what I did achieve at the Herrenhof was a certain connection with the Castle."

Writing like this cannot be defended on the grounds that the novel recounts a dream, or that the need for indeterminacy dictates it. It is simply inchoate, tedious, and only to be understood on the grounds that Kafka himself did not wish it to be published, had not revised it, and thought (however ambiguously) that it deserved only to be burned. For there is page after page, not quite of this quality, but nevertheless of such lengthy and involved sentences, such repetitions of "zwar . . . aber, allerdings, übrigens, freilich," as no serious writer could allow himself.

The style has set in well before Olga's narrative about the Sortini episode. Long passages of monologue reported in indirect speech, involving the subjunctive, are a wearisome feature as early as chapter 13, and they continue sporadically for the remainder of the novel. Here is the child Hans Brunswick, recalling how K. addressed a question to his mother shortly after his first arrival—the absence of the subjunctive in the English makes it appear a little lighter than it really is:

> Hans's father had been very annoyed at the time about K., and would certainly never allow K. to visit his mother; indeed, he had wanted to seek K. out at the time, to punish him for his behaviour, and only his mother had prevented that. But above all his mother herself in general wanted to speak to nobody, and her question about K. was no exception to the rule, on the contrary, just on the very occasion of his being mentioned she would have been able to express a wish to see him, but she had not done so, and thereby clearly expressed her will.

If it were not a child whose words were being reported (by Kafka, not by any intermediary character) one might suppose this to be a parody, humorously intended, of the official jargon likely to be heard at the Castle. But since a small boy is the supposed speaker one can only conclude that Kafka has succumbed himself to the weakness.

Only a man imbued with officialese and occasionally unable to shake free of it in his creative writing could write so often such sentences as these:

> But with regard to the most serious deficiencies, the inadequate provision for sleeping and heating, she promised without fail some relief for the following day.

> The teacher would gladly have let the cat stay there, but an allusion relating to this was decisively rejected by the schoolmistress with a reference to the cruelty of K.

The frequency of words like "somewhere," "somehow," "somebody," reinforce the general feeling of indeterminacy.

The writing in the second half of the book is inferior to that in the first half, and this may be partly due (if my presumption is right) to a determination to make the figures of Klamm and Sortini, in their symbolical functions, coalesce. Yet it would be quite wrong to conclude that the second half fulfilled none of the promise of the first. Some dogged reading is needed, to get through the Hans Brunswick and Amalia episodes, but in the final chapters (omitted by Max Brod from the earliest edition, and so not included in the first English translation) remarkable developments take place. I am thinking of the episode with the official Bürgel, and of the scenes which follow before the final pages peter out.

The meeting with Bürgel is not unlike the meeting with the prison-chaplain in *The Trial*. It comes at a climactic moment fairly near the end. K.'s whole situation is outlined to him by a person in authority, and he is for the first time given some assurance, however slight, about his position. As in so many cases, however, *The Castle* reverses the situation of *The Trial*. Where the chaplain seems concerned first to show K. that he has no chance of ever getting anywhere, then to confuse him completely, Bürgel seems to offer a real chance of success, which only K.'s somnolence prevents him from taking. All the confusion seems to have led, by virtue of the very fact that it is confusion, stumblingly, blindly, with no proper awareness of how it has come about, to a solution which, if accepted, would give K. all he ever looked for. It is a paradoxical solution, to be sure, yet a solution for all that. And all K. does is to fall asleep at the crucial moment. So the question that must arise, considering the vagueness of a good deal of what has gone before, is whether the climactic offer has any significance, or whether it is advanced merely to be dismissed as easily as other things are in the novel, on no particular grounds except a general readiness to be frustrated.

One striking thing about the Bürgel interview is that there is almost direct communication between two characters. In many parts of the novel there are monologues, and in this one also the main purpose is to expound a situation, indicating doubts and hesitations, and the usual obsessive words occur frequently here also. The difference is that Bürgel seems himself to be genuinely involved, and that he is offering a course of action which K. may at any moment adopt, so that the whole scene gains in dramatic tension. Bürgel is telling K., of course, that the situation he finds himself in at this instant is the only one that can really lead to success. K. has stumbled at night and by accident—not taking any advantage, then—into the room of an official not allocated to his particular case, and it is only in such an event that an official feels compelled to grant any request that the applicant may make. He does not tell K. this directly, but only obliquely, outlining a situation exactly like K.'s at this present moment, yet never saying openly that he, Bürgel, will grant any request K. makes, so that the whole interview begins to feel like a game of chess in which many pieces are *en prise,* and a single move will suddenly unfold incalculable possibilities. In fact Bürgel describes the situation in terms suggesting a kind of Hegelian intensification on both sides. (In Hegel's philosophy man is seen as "alienated" ("entfremdet") from the Spirit that moves all things by virtue of the fact that he is a mere individual, whereas the Spirit is "the All," or at least manifests itself as the All, even though essentially it is nothing. The greater this alienation becomes, and the more it is intensified, the greater is the tendency for it to suffer a reversal and to reassume a total identity with the Spirit. Thus the man in whom alienation is complete—one thinks, if one is Hegel, of Christ's words of forsakenness on the Cross—is the man most nearly at one with the Whole.) The more weary, disappointed and indifferent the applicant is, the greater is the desire of the official to help him, and for the official, at any rate, there are overtones suggesting that he acquires supreme power at such a moment: the official, Bürgel says, violently seizes "a promotion in rank exceeding all conception." There is a strong suggestion here that the official takes on quasi-divine powers at such a moment, while the applicant in his dejection seems at least to resemble such a man as de Caussade describes in his treatise on mystical prayer: "This soul [in whom God lives] often enough, is abandoned in a corner, like a bit of broken pottery which no one imagines to be of any use. Thus abandoned by creatures, but experiencing Godly and very real, true and active love, though it is a love infused in repose, this soul does not apply itself to anything by its own movement; all it can do is to abandon itself and surrender itself into God's hands, to serve him in ways known to him" (*Abandon à la divine providence*).

It is quite common in treatises on mysticism to associate the ultimate dereliction of the soul, the moment when it feels itself completely abandoned, with the highest state to which that soul can attain—in fact it is one of the potential evils of mysticism, that it holds out such enormous promise as the reward of such total loss.

But Bürgel is not represented as divine in any Christian sense, nor does he seem to feel any love for K., nor does K. seem to feel any love for him or anyone else. The whole scene is inverted, in comparison with orthodox Christian mysticism. Bürgel is only telling K. all this because he himself wants to go to sleep, and thinks he can talk himself into that state. He can scarcely be using a loving irony—that is, deliberately refraining from putting K. into a too knowing position out of care lest K. succumb to a "temptation on the mountain-top"—judging by the way he exuberantly stretches himself as soon as the interview has to stop (there is something almost devilish in his glee here), and as K. goes he is really more concerned to assure him that nothing could have been done after all, than to lament his lack of success. There is something evil about Bürgel altogether, not so much in the way he speaks of normal interviews as ending more or less automatically in the defeat of the applicant—this is the first official confirmation K. has had, that the Castle is more bent on procrastination than anything else—as in the way he speaks of wanting to resist the temptation to do the applicant some good. "When the applicant is in the room, it's already pretty bad, it's true. It presses on your heart. 'How long will you be able to resist?' you ask yourself. But there simply will not be any resistance, you know that." There is passion in his desire to meet the applicant, "a real thirst," he says, to suffer the applicant's useless demands along with him. And there is desperation, because one knows that the applicant's request will have to be granted, even though "at least so far as one can see, it will well and truly tear down the whole official organisation." Close though this situation is to that of some traditional mysticism, Bürgel is claiming to speak on behalf of an organisation that is opposed to the granting of any request, and which, so far as he (or the reader) knows, can even be destroyed by an action of its own inspired by an act of charitable sympathy. Hence the obliqueness, the sly presenting of K.'s own situation without actually pointing to the obvious parallel, the failure actually to make the offer which Bürgel says he is unable to resist making. Bürgel sees the whole position not as an opportunity for love, but as one in which he would undergo something like murder or rape:

> "The applicant, like a robber in a forest, forces sacrifices
> from us that we should never be capable of otherwise; very
> well, so it feels at the moment, while the applicant is

before us, strengthening us and forcing us and encouraging us, and while everything is going on half unreflectively; but what will it be like afterwards, when it is all over, and the applicant, satiated and unworried, leaves us, and we stand there, alone, defenceless at the misuse of our office— the whole thing is past thinking of! And nevertheless we are happy. How suicidal happiness can be."

It is as though K. had penetrated to the Will itself (in Schopenhauer's sense), to the very quick of life, and found it as ruthlessly bent on destruction as ever the Court was in *The Trial,* even to the point of deeply desiring its own death through the means of doing what is normally accounted good. Bürgel is offering K., however obliquely, the means of destroying him, and it is, presumably, a destruction he would welcome, as Joseph K. welcomed his execution. That *is* the way of the world, as Bürgel would have it: a kind of sexual relationship in which one partner is misused—and likes it—rather than a free giving and taking on each side.

Yet, such is the uncertainty about values in the whole work, it is not completely clear that Bürgel is wrong, or evil, in his unwillingness to grant a request made by an applicant such as K. If he sees that being in a cosmically dominant position is of no benefit to a man, he may be in the right to show such unwillingness. The trouble is, one does not know where Bürgel stands or what he makes of all this. The uncertainty is ingrained in the novel: it is not a quality for admiration, though attempts at interpretation lead one into subtleties; it is rather that the novel has no guiding centre, nothing by which to see how it may be read with a real sense of meeting the author.

And K. is too tired to do anything about Bürgel's offer. There is no virtue here. K. has made no progress in virtue since the beginning of the novel: despite apparent parallels there is no reason for thinking of him in terms of a Christian mystic who has arrived in a comparable state of dereliction after constant prayer and exercise. And in failing to take advantage of Bürgel's offer K. is not sizing it up, declining to do anything for this reason or that, he is simply very tired, and has "a great disinclination for things that concerned him." The sense of this extraordinary spiritual climax—that really is what it amounts to, however strange to tradition it may be—is not contained in any moral progress, but in the words of Bürgel just before K. leaves:

> "Go then, what do you want here? No, don't excuse yourself on account of your sleepiness, whatever for? The vital spark only reaches certain limits, who can help it if this limit is significant in a different way too? No, nobody can. That is how the world corrects itself and maintains its balance. It is an excellent, an unimaginably excellent arrangement, though in another respect it is comfortless.
>   . . . Go then; who knows what awaits you over there [in Erlanger's room], there's no end of opportunities in this place. The only thing is, of course, that there are some opportunities that in a certain sense are too big to be made use of, there are things that collapse on account of nothing else but themselves."

The inference is that Bürgel was perfectly safe in making his oblique offer to K. Precisely because K. was so over-tired, disappointed and indifferent, he could not take up the offer: only by pursuing his goal with such energy that he became weary and indifferent could he ever have reached a position where he could put the vital question (whatever that might be), and so the one thing cancels out the other, the supreme command is at the mercy of the one man who cannot use it. That is how the world (Bürgel surprisingly says, but one sees his drift) goes on existing, because, as I interpret, it is an evil world in which the desire for destruction, the Schopenhauerian Will to extinction, is always predominant and even manages to incorporate "the good" in its destructive process, even manages to survive when its whole nature is bent on vanishing out of existence.

If it were possible to speak of a fallen angel, in the context of this novel, Bürgel would fit the case very well. There is in him all the remaining desire to do good which one would imagine a former spirit in heaven to have, and it amounts to a passion, even now. Yet there is nothing in him that will actively seek to realise this good, he is acquiescent in the frustration which the whole organisation imposes, and shows every sign of delight when Erlanger's summons breaks off the interview before K. is able to put the situation to his own use.

"We are digging the pit of Babel," Kafka observed in his diaries. Not the tower which challenged heaven and brought destruction on itself *that* way, but the pit which moves further and further down into dereliction and hopelessness, without the saving grace of the traditional mystic's continuing love, and which ultimately wants nothing but a destructive union with the all-annihilating Will.

But this strange climax, or, in a special sense, anti-climax, is not the end of the novel. There remains K.'s brief encounter with Erlanger and his witnessing of the distribution of the documents, and finally his return to the barmaid Pepi in the inn, and all this seems to prolong the moment in which a paradoxical achievement is being celebrated. K. has got nowhere, of course, in the terms outlined by Bürgel, and the futility of it all seems to be stressed by Erlanger's injunction to K. to see that Frieda returns to the service of Klamm, an injunction which K. has no means of fulfilling since Frieda has abandoned him for Jeremias. (Milena similarly broke off the relation with Kafka after some time.) But the terms outlined by Bürgel need not necessarily be admirable. When he tells K. that he could "control everything" he may very well recall the temptation of Christ by Satan with the offer of dominion over all the world. There is no need to assume that Bürgel or indeed the Castle itself stands for anything good, despite the hints at divinity in Klamm: gods are not necessarily good. If K. had made a positive rejection of Bürgel's offer, instead of falling asleep, he would have made for an unambiguous conclusion.

There is no such unambiguity, at least in the last chapter, but one (chap. 19). After meeting Erlanger, K. is left alone in the corridor while various documents are being handed out, and for the whole of the chapter a series of suggestions and counter-suggestions is made. K. reflects first on the officials behind the office-doors, and surmises that, though no doubt tired, they are enjoying "indestructible quiet, indestructible peace. 'If one is weary a little at midday, that is all part of the natural and happy course of the day. These gentlemen have continual midday,' K. said to himself." And this is an important reflection, if one thinks of how often Kafka spoke in his diaries of "the Indestructible": it is one of the most striking concepts that he uses. Yet as Kafka goes on, in the next sentence, there appears a lighthearted element in the mood, which disturbs any normal notion of peace and quiet. It is not simply that the pleasure is childlike:

> "The babble of voices in these rooms had something extremely joyful about it. At one moment it sounded like the rejoicing of children getting ready for an excursion, at another like the first stirrings in a hen-coop, like the joy of being in complete accord with the awakening day; somewhere one of the gentlemen even imitated the crowing of a cock."

—it is rather that this crowing like a cock (a sound which carries overtones of Peter's denial of Christ as well as of daybreak—both the depths of disgrace and the announcement of a new era) heralds a whole series of actions that are childlike to the point of zaniness. The officials are petulant, refractory, impatient, they stamp their feet, clap their hands, keep shouting the number of the file they want; one pours a basin of water over one of the distributing clerks, another throws a whole file over the partition-wall so that its contents spill all over the floor, others refuse to open their doors at all, despite repeated shoulder-charges. It is all like a mad cartoon, or some Chaplinesque comedy, and quite amusing in its way, though it turns K.'s benevolent reflections on the officials' serenity into nonsense. They are behaving like Bürgel, more than like the people K. supposes them to be. Yet that point about indestructibility seemed to have a special significance, coming just after the climactic interview.

Then again, K. witnesses the moment when the chief distributing clerk, having got rid of all his files, is left with one small scrap of paper, which has somehow come adrift, and which the clerk destroys apparently because he does not know what else to do with it. "That might very well be mine," is K.'s comment, and whether it is or is not, the comment has the effect of drawing attention to the possibility that K.'s case is now over and done with. It is only a possibility. K. does not know, and Kafka does not tell us, whether the document is his. If it is, there is still no telling whether it has been destroyed simply because the clerk is impatient, or because K.'s case has been dismissed, and if it has been dismissed, whether this is because he is beneath contempt or above reproach. All the same, the possibility is there, that his case, the Bürgel interview being finished, is now over and done with.

This possibility is then reinforced, though still ambiguously, by the behaviour of the officials as soon as the clerk has left. One begins to press his electric bell, others join in, and soon there are so many bells going that they seem to be expressing not some need for help, but "an excess of joy" and even to be celebrating a victory, though it is not said what victory, and the idea of *electric* bells doing this, as distinct from church bells, is not too easy to grasp. K. soon learns what the ringing means from the landlord and landlady, who come running in comic haste to answer the summons of the bells, and who explain to K. very forcefully that it is only his presence in the corridor that has caused all the trouble. The officials have had too much delicacy to require K. to leave, but so long as he was present the distribution of files could not take place in due order, and only now, when the distribution is over, have the officials decided to have him sent away. This explanation is unsatisfying. The officials have shown no sign of delicacy; they have behaved more like spoiled children than men of tact, and K. ought to have no difficulty in pointing this out. That he does not do so may be due to Kafka's determination—conscious or otherwise—not to allow any positive suggestion that is not immediately negatived. But the fact is, the landlord simply does not negative what the reader has seen: the officials remain foolish from start to finish, and nothing they have done suggests any sensitivity or decent shame at having their private behaviour scrutinised—on the contrary, they have made an exhibition of themselves before K.'s eyes. So the bare thread of sense that could perhaps be observed running through the various events is turned into nonsense. If one takes the view that K. has done well (though not virtuously well) in not falling for Bürgel's offer of power, that he then comes to see the officials in a more positively good light, that as a result of all this his file disappears, or is abolished, and that the officials celebrate this by ringing their bells, one has at any rate a logical sequence of events to point to. On the other hand, the notion that K. is deceived about the indestructible peace, that the officials are glad to see the back of him, and that, though not sensitive as the landlord makes out, they are more likely to rejoice at the death—or at least frustration—of a sinner, than at anything else, is really more potent. So far as the Castle is concerned, it seems, K.'s case is finished, and that is the victory that is being celebrated.

Yet, given the nature of the Castle as it has appeared especially in the latter half of the novel, that would not be at all a bad thing. All this ceaseless attempt at penetrating to the innermost depths and conquering them, has characterised European thinking, or a good deal of it, for a very long time. So long, that failure to enter the Castle, failure to dominate, is easily taken as a sign of a defeat worse than any other that could be imagined. Yet, given the nature of K.'s Castle, the shifting image as he has seen it, there is no need to see defeat as a loss. Ceasing to have dealings with an organisation like this is rather a gain, and if K.'s document has in fact been destroyed, so much the better, one may say, whatever the officials and the landlord may think about it. This moment in the novel is rather like the moment in "In the Penal Colony," when the machine of torture breaks into pieces. The machine seemed to be a means of enlightenment, as the Castle seemed to K., yet when placed to the final test it could only break down. Is it the same here, or roughly the same—has not K.'s potential challenge to the Castle reached its maximum, so that now only a complete severance is possible?

If Kafka had been fully conscious of that implication, he might have been able to finish the novel. In fact, it is doubtful whether he had more than an unconscious grasp of it; in other words, his mind, groping in darkness, deliberately remaining "unknowing," not planning out the novel in advance, but following where his torments took him, went as far as to outline a kind of parody of deliverance, a parody that still belongs to the world of the Castle and is still at best an inversion of real deliverance. Real deliverance, Kafka himself knew, was to know the indestructible in oneself and not to strain after it, to let it be, as he wrote in his aphorisms. This he could not do within the novel without straining to breaking-point his integrity: this work, to remain whole as a work of art, had to continue as it had begun and developed, for once the Bürgel interview had taken place the die was cast, the dominant evil in the Castle had irrevocably made its mark. Had K. accepted Bürgel's offer it would have been like a pact with evil, on which there was no going back. But his failure to accept was not a refusal, it was merely a weariness of spirit, and his lack of interest in "things that concerned himself" was not a choice, not a real self-denial, but a drifting, quietistic absence of self-regard. A sane man, however self-denying he may be, must have that essential self-regard, or the quick of life in him dies. In K. it has very nearly died, as the novel draws to an end.

That Kafka is still not, as an artist, a free man, is shown by the tedium of the final chapter, at least for the first twenty pages, a stream of hesitations and modifications, denials and concessions, which run on without so much as a paragraph division. We are back again, after the comparatively lively sequence of events since K. first entered Bürgel's room, in a world of "indeed," "probably," "it is true . . ." and "for that matter." They are not K.'s words, and this makes an important difference. They are the words of Pepi, the barmaid who has succeeded Frieda temporarily in the tap-room at the Bridge Inn, and who now prattles on with a self-indulgence which must be ascribed in some part to Kafka too, since he seems to have abandoned all control as a novelist in order to give Pepi her head. And yet, despite the tedium, one can just see, even within Kafka's abandonment to the darkness, a glimmer of acceptable sense. Pepi's sole preoccupation is with herself, her prospects of promotion within the hierarchy, her jealousy of Frieda's relation with Klamm, her conviction that she could do better. She is self-regard personified, one might say. And the curious fact is that her name is like one used so often by Kafka for his fictional *alter egos* that it must surely have been significant to him. One could have done with more of an indication than this rather obscure one, it is true. Yet there it is: Pepi is the usual abbreviation or nickname for girls called Josephine, and Joseph is not only the name of K.'s counterpart in *The Trial,* it is also the name given by K. in *The Castle* on one occasion, though he is not otherwise referred to except by his initial; Josephine is also of course the name of the singing mouse in the short story which seems meant to comment ironically on Kafka's (and other writers') artistic pretensions. So it is not at all improbable that Kafka had in mind, in introducing Pepi, a confrontation of himself by Joseph K. Here all K.'s determination to get on, to reach the highest point, and enter the Castle, is parodied—or perhaps "reflected" is the better word, when the manifest intention is so slight—in the figure of this childish young woman whose absurdities become more and more unbearably apparent as her monologue (much of it, like Hans Brunswick's, in the form of reported speech) continues.

Kafka does not control this. Yet K., confronted, as it were, with this caricature of himself, does remain remarkably calm and sane. Whatever the truth may be about the document and the behaviour of the officials—a truth so smudged over with unrefuted absurdities that all discussion of it must remain in confusion—it does seem at least very likely that the unconscious process which brought Kafka to write of the destruction of the document had been a move towards liberation of some sort, even though it was still much less than a full liberation. It is moving to find K. using words like these, when Pepi has been complaining that both he and she have been deceived, since it reflects back on K.'s earlier gratification at having his hopes frustrated:

> "So long as you go on complaining about being deceived," said K., "I can't come to any agreement with you. You always want to make out you have been deceived, because it flatters you, and because it moves you. But the truth is, you are not suited to this job. How clearly unfitted you must be, if a man like me, who in your opinion is more ignorant than anyone, can see it."

Again, K.'s friendly criticism of Pepi's absurd costume, telling her that she dresses up like an angel, or as she thinks angels are, because of her overwheening pretensions, strikes an unusually humble note, besides reintroducing the religious note that has been absent for some time.

Similarly, K.'s lack of jealousy towards Klamm shows a new generosity in him that can surely only be the fruit of some deep-seated change. But though there is humility and generosity not only in this, but in several other of K.'s observations to Pepi, the change is still only partial, and his ideals still remain as much concerned with gaining power as ever. In contrasting Pepi with Frieda, K. shows that he is concerned with some kind of moral values, but they are still the values associated with his old determination to pursue and destroy Klamm:

> "Have you ever noticed her eyes?" K. asks Pepi. "Those weren't the eyes of a barmaid, they were very nearly the eyes of a landlady. She saw everything, and yet each individual at the same time, and the look she kept for a single individual was still strong enough to dominate him."

The odd idea of a hierarchy in the tap-room comes as near explicitness here as it ever does: one wonders just what landladies' eyes do look like. But the essential point is still this admiration for power, for the ability to subject a lover to oneself, which seems to have been in K. from the start, and which runs alongside his praise of Frieda's matter-of-factness and equanimity.

There is, then, a remarkable change in K., something that has no parallel in *The Trial* or in any other of Kafka's works, and this change has come about not through any conscious willing, though the strange unconscious process by which it is reached is detectable. He is now more generous, not vindictive or jealous at all, more willing to believe in other people's superiority to himself, and in the ineptitude of his approach to the Castle, than he was at the beginning, and all this comes at a point when he may (or may not— the issue is not one that can ever find an answer) have had all relationship with the Castle severed, when he has ceased to seek either to penetrate or to destroy it. The game of attack and counter-attack is over, and in these circumstances K. emerges a different man.

But the sense of frustration which still continues is due to K.'s continuing preoccupation with Pepi, if Pepi represents, as I have suggested, a kind of *alter ego*. K. can confront this caricature of himself that comes looming up out of the depths at him, but he has no alternative but to go down into them with her. Pepi's underground quarters are constricting, if cosy, and the suggestive overtones they carry must be obvious enough. K. will not move out into a freer world by joining Pepi, as he now half proposes to do: at most he will confront his own self without continual self-laceration, an achievement he may be glad to settle for. It may even be that he will not stay there for good. Pepi, it seems, is bound to the underground room, which is scarcely a statement to take absolutely literally. K., on the other hand, may leave when spring comes, he is bound only for the winter, and again a parallel from Rilke comes to mind:

> Doch unter Wintern ist einer so endlos Winter,
> Daß überwinternd dein Herz überhaupt übersteht.

(But among all winters there is one that's so endlessly winter, that outwintering it your heart will outlast.)

There is a part of K., at least, which may rise again, but that is the briefest of hints, scarcely even a speculation. Essentially, K. has emerged from the quest for the Castle with only death in sight, and a bare hope of something beyond. Equally important, the writing continues as it has been through the greater part of the novel, fluid, incessantly conceding and retreating from all definiteness of statement, never differentiating between characters (or only minimally: the Superintendent is rather more inclined to use jargon than others are), spreading a mist of doubt which is there not because doubt is justified but because it has become a regular principle to deny whatever is affirmed. Momentarily, towards the end, Kafka seems on the point of abandoning this principle, which is the principle of the Castle itself. But because the movement of the novel is dreamlike, the conscious recognition can never be made. To have recognised where the undertow of the dream was taking him, Kafka would have had to wake up, and to have woken up would have destroyed the unity of the novel, or rather the uniformity, the oppressive nightmarish repetitiveness which is the kind of unity it has. The character he has created can only go on to meet the now sinister landlady, with her half-promise to "come and fetch him" next day, and then to the old crouching figure of Gerstäcker's mother (in the final fragment released by Max Brod for the later editions), in whom the breath of corruption almost touches him. The novel breaks off in midsentence, probably because Kafka could not take it relentlessly on to the deathliness which was all he had left for K. Yet there has been sufficient indication of a reversal even within the uncontrollable dream, even in the quietistically acquiescent K. who perseveres only in acquiescence. One glimpses the truth in Hölderlin's lines:

> Herrscht im schiefesten Orkus
> Nicht ein Grades, ein Recht noch auch?

(Even in most crooked Hades, does not a straightness, a rightness prevail?)

Kafka's novel takes the reader a long way down into the hopelessness of Orcus, but though it never, so far as its own content is concerned, lets him emerge again, it does suggest a dull, yet insistent pull towards the reversal of all the values the Castle stands for. More than that one can't claim on its behalf. It did not take Kafka to the reversal of fortunes he sometimes looked for, and it will not, of itself, help any reader there either.

The Castle: A Company of Gnostic Demons

Erich Heller

The relationship of Kafka's heroes to that truth for which they so
desperately search can best be seen in the image through which Plato,
in a famous passage of his *Republic,* expresses man's pitiable ignorance about the true nature of the Ideas. Chained to the ground of his
cave, with his back towards the light, all he perceives of the
fundamental reality of the world is a play of shadows thrown on the
wall of his prison. But for Kafka there is a further complication:
perfectly aware of his wretched imprisonment and obsessed with a
monomaniac desire to know, the prisoner has, by his unruly
behaviour and his incessant entreaties, provoked the government of
his prison to an act of malicious generosity. In order to satisfy this
passion for knowledge they have covered the walls with mirrors
which, owing to the curved surface of the cave, distort what they
reflect. Now the prisoner sees lucid pictures, definite shapes, clearly
recognizable faces, an inexhaustible wealth of detail. His gaze is fixed
no longer on empty shades, but on a full reflection of ideal reality.
Face to face with the images of Truth, he is yet doubly agonized by
their hopeless distortion. With an unparalleled fury of pedantry he
observes the curve of every line, the ever-changing countenance of
every figure, drawing schemes of every possible aberration from
reality which his mirror may cause, making now this angle and now
that the basis of his endless calculations which, he passionately

From *Kafka.* © 1974 by Erich Heller. William Collins Sons & Co., Ltd., 1974. All
translations of *Das Schloss* are by Willa and Edwin Muir.

hopes, will finally yield the geometry of truth or of that necessity which sometimes he opposed to the notion of truth.

In a letter (December 16, 1911) Kafka says: "I am separated from all things by a hollow space, and I do not even reach to its boundaries." In another (November 19, 1913): "Everything appears to me construed. . . . I am chasing after constructions. I enter a room, and I find them in a corner, a white tangle." On October 21, 1921, he enters in his diary: "All is imaginary—family, office, friends, the street, all imaginary, far away or close at hand, the woman; the truth that lies closest, however, is only this: that you are beating your head against the wall of a windowless and doorless cell." And in one of his "Reflections on Sin, Pain, Hope and the True Way" he writes: "Our art is a dazzled blindness before the truth: The light on the grotesque recoiling mask is true, but nothing else."

Kafka's novels take place in infinity. Yet their atmosphere is as oppressive as that of those unaired rooms in which so many of their scenes are enacted. For infinity is incompletely defined as the ideal point where two parallels meet. There is yet another place where they come together: the distorting mirror. Thus they carry into the prison of their violently distorted union the agony of infinite separation.

It is a Tantalus situation, and in Kafka's work the ancient curse has come to life once more. Kafka says of himself (in the sequence of the aphorisms "He" contained in the volume *The Great Wall of China*): "He is thirsty, and is cut off from a spring by a mere clump of bushes. But he is divided against himself: one part overlooks the whole, sees that he is standing here and that the spring is just beside him; but another part notices nothing, has at most a divination that the first part sees all. But as he notices nothing he cannot drink." Indeed, it was a curse, and not a word of light, which called the universe of Kafka's novels into existence. The very clay from which it was made bore the imprint of a malediction before any creature had touched it. He builds to a splendid design, but the curse runs like a vein through every stone. In one of his most revealing parables, in the Fourth Octavo Note-Book (included in the volume *Dearest Father*), Kafka shows himself aware of this:

> Everything fell in with his intention and contributed to the building. Foreign workers brought the blocks of marble, already hewn and ready to be fitted together. In accordance

with the indication, given by his moving finger, the blocks rose up and shifted into place. No building ever rose into being as easily as this temple did, or rather, this temple came into being in the true manner of temples. Only on every block—from what quarry did they come?—there were clumsy scribblings by senseless childish hands, or rather, entries made by barbaric mountain-dwellers in order to annoy or to deface or to destroy completely, scratched into the stone with instruments that were obviously magnificently sharp, intended to endure for an eternity that would outlast the temple.

It is the reality of the curse that constitutes the ruthlessly compelling logic of Kafka's writings. If they defy all attempts to interpret them in a simple, straightforward manner, this is because he never thinks, or imagines, in disputable or refutable generalities. His thinking is a reflex movement of his being and shares the irrefutability of all that is. And it is at an infinite number of removes from the Cartesian *Cogito ergo sum.* Indeed, it sometimes seems that an unknown "It" does all the thinking that matters, the radius of its thought touching the circumference of Kafka's existence here and there, causing him infinite pain, bringing his life into question and promising salvation on one condition only: that he should expand his being to bring it within the orbit of that strange intelligence. The formula has become: "It thinks, and therefore I am not," with only the agony of despair providing overpowering proof that he is alive.

There is, outside this agony, no reality about which he could entertain or communicate thoughts, nothing apart from the curse of his own separation from that intelligence. Yet it is a complete world that is to be found within that pain, the exact pattern of creation once more, but this time made of the stuff of which curses are made. Like sorrow in the Tenth of Rilke's *Duino Elegies,* despair is given a home of its own in Kafka's works, faithfully made in the image of customary life, but animated by the blast of the curse. Never before has absolute darkness been represented with so much clarity, and the very madness of desperation with so much composure and sobriety. In his work an intolerable spiritual pride is expressed with the legitimate and convincing gesture of humility, disintegration finds its own level of integrity, and impenetrable complexity an all but *sancta simplicitas.* Kafka strives to discover the moral law of a boundlessly deceitful world, and performs in a totally incalculable domain, ruled by evil demons, the most precise mathematical measurements.

It has been said that *The Castle* is a religious allegory, a kind of modern *Pilgrim's Progress,* indeed that the unattainable building is the abode of divine law and divine grace. This would seem to be not only a misapprehension reflecting a profound religious confusion, but an indication of the loss of all sureness of religious discrimination. Where there is a spiritual famine, *anything* that is of the spirit may taste like bread from Heaven, and minds imbued with psychology and "comparative religion" may find the difference negligible between Prometheus clamped to the rock, and the martyrdom of a Christian saint; between an ancient curse and the grace that makes a new man.

The Castle is as much a religious allegory as a photographic likeness of the Devil in person could be said to be an allegory of Evil. Every allegory has an opening into the rarefied air of abstractions, and is furnished with signposts pointing to an ideal concept beyond. But *The Castle* is a terminus of soul and mind, a *non plus ultra* of existence. In an allegory the author plays a kind of guessing game with his reader, if he does not actually provide the answers himself; but there is no key to *The Castle*. It is true to say that its reality does not precisely correspond to what is commonly understood in the "positive" world as real, namely, neutral sense-perceptions of objects and, neatly separated from them, feelings. (Hence our most authentic and realistic intellectual pursuits: natural sciences and psychology; and our besetting sins: the ruthlessness of acquisitive techniques and sentimentality). In Kafka's novels there is no such division between the external sphere and the domain of inwardness, and therefore no such reality. There is only the tragic mythology of the absolutely incongruous relationship between the two worlds.

Kafka's creations are at the opposite pole to the writings of that type of Romantic poet, the true poetical representative of the utilitarian age, who distils from a spiritually more and more sterile external reality those elements which are still of some use to the emotions, or else withdraws from its barren fields into the greenhouse vegetation of inwardness. The author of *The Castle* does not select for evocative purposes, nor does he project his inner experience into carefully chosen timeless settings. He does not, after the manner of Joyce, give away, in the melodious flow of intermittent articulation, the secret bedroom conversations which self conducts with self. There are no private symbols in his work, such as would be found in symbolist writing, no crystallized fragments of inner sensations charged with mysterious significance; nor is there, after the fashion of the Expressionists, any rehearsing of new gestures of the soul, meant to be more in harmony with the new rhythm of modern society. Instead of all this, the reader is faced with the shocking spectacle of a miraculously sensitive soul incapable of being either reasonable, or cynical, or resigned, or rebellious, about the prospect of eternal damnation. The world which this soul perceives is unmistakably like the reader's own: a castle that is a castle and "symbolizes" merely what all castles symbolize: power and authority; a bureaucracy drowning in a deluge of forms and files; an obscure hierarchy of officialdom making it impossible ever to find the man authorized to deal with a particular case; officials who work overtime and yet get nowhere; numberless interviews which never are to the point; inns where the peasants meet, and barmaids who serve the officials. In fact, it is an excruciatingly familiar world, but reproduced by a creative intelligence which is endowed with the knowledge that it is a world damned for ever. Shakespeare once made one of his characters say: "They say miracles are past, and we have our philosophical persons, to make modern and familiar things supernatural and causeless. Hence it is that we make trifles of terrors, ensconcing ourselves in seeming knowledge when we should submit ourselves to an unknown fear." In Kafka we have the abdication of the philosophical persons.

In Kafka's work the terror recaptures the trifles, and the unknown fear invades all seeming knowledge—particularly that of psychology. Even the most mistaken religious interpretations of Kafka's writings show at least an awareness of its religious character, whereas the psychological analyses, in their devastating plausibility, tend to reduce them to symptoms of the Oedipus complex. Certainly, there cannot be the slightest doubt that Kafka's relationship to his father was exceedingly strained; but only one son, among the many unable to come to terms with their fathers, has written *The Castle*. To interpret this or any other novel of Kafka's in the perspective of the Oedipus complex is about as helpful to our understanding of his work as the statement that Kafka would have been a different person (and perhaps not a writer at all) if he had had another father: a thought, of which even psychologically less initiated ages might have been capable if they had deemed it worth thinking. This kind of pyschology can contribute as much to the explanation of a work of art as ornithological anatomy to the comprehension of what the nightingale's song meant to Keats. But so deeply engrained is psychology in the epoch's sensibility that most readers, even when they are moved by the autonomous reality which the author has created, soon regain the balance of mind required for its "reduction," its translation into what it "really" means; and by that they mean precisely that meaningless experience which the artist has succeeded in transcending through his poetic creation. If, for instance, the writer believes he has discovered the meaning of his senselessly tormenting feud with his father—a discovery he has made in creating his work—; that he should find his place within a true spiritual order of divine authority, the psychological reader will insist that, by talking about God, the author "really" means his father.

In Kafka we have before us the modern mind, seemingly self-sufficient, intelligent, sceptical, ironical, splendidly trained for the great game of pretending that the world it comprehends in sterilized sobriety is the only and ultimate reality there is—yet a mind living in sin with the soul of Abraham. Thus he knows two things at once, and both with equal assurance: that there is no God, and that there must be God. It is the perspective of the curse: the intellect dreaming its dream of absolute freedom, and the soul knowing of its terrible bondage. The conviction of damnation is all that is left of faith, standing out like a rock in a landscape the softer soil of which has been eroded by the critical intellect. Kafka once said (in the Fourth Octavo Note-Book): "I should welcome eternity, and when I do find it I am sad."

This is merely an exhausted echo of the fanfares of despair with which Nietzsche, who had some share in Kafka's intellectual education and is, beyond any question of influence, in many respects one of his spiritual ancestors, welcomed his vision of eternity. In one of the posthumously published notes on *Zarathustra* he says about his idea of the Eternal Recurrence: "We have produced the hardest possible thought—now let us create the creature who will accept it lightheartedly and blissfully!": the *Übermensch*. He conceived the Eternal Recurrence as a kind of spiritualized Darwinian test to select for survival the spiritually fittest. This he formulated with the utmost precision: "I perform the great experiment: who can bear the idea of Eternal Recurrence?" And an even deeper insight into the anatomy of despair we gain from Nietzsche's posthumous aphorisms and epigrams which were assembled by his editors in the two volumes of *The Will to Power*, many of which refer to the idea of Eternal Recurrence: "Let us consider this idea in its most terrifying form: existence, as it is, without meaning or goal, but inescapably recurrent, without a finale into nothingness." Nietzsche's *Übermensch* is the creature strong enough to live forever a cursed existence, even to derive from it the Dionysian raptures of tragic acceptance. Nietzsche feels certain that only the *Übermensch* could be equal to the horror of a senseless eternity, and perform the great metamorphosis of turning this "most terrifying" knowledge into the terror of superhuman delight. And Kafka? On most of the few occasions when, in his diary, he speaks of happiness he registers it as the result of a transformation of torture into bliss as in those horrible diary entries such as (November 2, 1911): "This morning, for the first time in a long time, the joy again of imagining a knife twisted in my heart." If Nietzsche's *Übermensch* is the visionary counterweight to the weight of the curse, then Kafka is its chosen victim. What sometimes has been interpreted as signs of a religious "breakthrough" in his later writings is merely the all-engulfing weariness of a Nietzschean Prometheus: in the fourth of his Prometheus legends (Fourth Octavo Note-Book) Kafka writes: "Everyone grew weary of the meaningless affair. The gods grew weary, the eagles grew weary, the wound closed wearily."

Thus Kafka's work, as much as Nietzsche's, must remain a stumbling-block to the analysing interpreter to whom, in the enlightened atmosphere of modernity, the word "curse" comes only as a faint memory of Greek tragedy, or as a figurative term for a combination of ill-luck and psychological maladjustments. Yet the grey world of Kafka's novels is luminous with its fire. To be sure, Kafka's *Castle* is, as has been held, about life in the grip of a power "which all religions have acknowledged"; but this power is not "divine law and divine grace," but rather one which, having rebelled against the first and fallen from the second, has, in its own domain, successfully contrived the suspension of both. Undoubtedly, the land-surveyor K., hero of *The Castle,* is religiously fascinated by its inscrutably horrid bureaucracy; but again it is a word from Nietzsche, and not from the Gospels, that sums up the situation: "Wretched man, your god lies in the dust, broken to fragments, and serpents dwell around him. And now you love even the serpents for his sake."

II

The Castle is not an allegorical, but a symbolic novel. A discussion of the difference could easily deteriorate into pedantry, the more so as, in common and literary usage, the terms are applied rather arbitrarily. It will, however, help our understanding of Kafka's work if we distinguish, in using these two terms, two different modes of experience and expression. I shall therefore define my own—not less arbitrary—use of these words.

The symbol is what it represents; the allegory represents what, in itself, it is *not*. The terms of reference of an allegory are abstractions; a symbol refers to something specific and concrete. The statue of a blindfolded woman, holding a pair of scales, is an *allegory* of Justice; bread and wine are, for the Christian communicant, *symbols* of the Body and Blood of Christ. Thus an allegory must always be rationally translatable; whether a symbol is translatable or not depends on the fundamental agreement of society on the question of what kind of experience, out of the endless range of possible human experience, it regards as significant. The possibility of allegorizing will only vanish with the last man capable of *thinking in abstractions* and of forming *images* of them; yet the validity of symbols depends not on rational operations, but on complex experiences in which thought and feeling merge in the act of spiritual comprehension. The sacramental symbols, for instance, would become incommunicable among a race of men who no longer regard the life, death and resurrection of Christ as spiritually relevant *facts*. An allegory, being the imaginary representation of something abstract, is, as it were, doubly unreal; whereas the symbol, in being what it represents, possesses a double reality.

Goethe, summing up in one line at the end of *Faust* II the mature experience of his life, attributes whatever permanent reality there may be in a transient world to its symbolic significance. What is, is only *real* in so far as it is symbolic. Earlier in his life he defined the "true symbol" as that "particular" which represents the "universal," not, however, "as a dream or shadow, but as the revelation of the unfathomable in a moment filled with life" [in *Maximen und Reflexionen*].

The predicament of the symbol in our age is caused by a split between "reality" and what it signifies. There is no more any commonly accepted symbolic or transcendent order of things. What the modern mind perceives as order is established through the tidy relationship between things themselves. In one word: the only conceivable order is positivist-scientific. If there still is a—no doubt, diminishing—demand for the fuller reality of the symbol, then it must be provided for by the unsolicited gifts of art. But in the sphere of art the symbolic substance, dismissed from its disciplined commitments to reality, dissolves into incoherence, ready to attach itself to any fragment of experience, invading it with irresistible power, so that a pair of boots, or a chair in the painter's attic, or a single tree on a slope which the poet passes, or an obscure inscription in a Venetian church, may suddenly become the precariously unstable centre of an otherwise unfocused universe. Since "the great words, from the time when what really happened was still visible, are no longer for us" (as Rilke put it in his "Requiem" for a young poet), the "little words" have to carry an excessive freight of symbolic significance. No wonder that they are slow in delivering it. They are all but incommunicable private symbols, established beyond any doubt as symbols by the quality and intensity of the imaginative experience that has brought them forth, but lacking any representative properties. Such is the economy of human consciousness that the positivist impoverishment of the one region produces anarchy in the other. In the end, atomic lawlessness is likely to prevail in both.

The intellectual foundation of every human society is a generally accepted model of reality. One of the major intellectual difficulties of human existence seems to be due to the fact that this model of reality is in every single case a mere *interpretation* of the world, and yet exerts, as long as it seems the valid interpretation, the subtly compelling claim to being accepted as the only true picture of the universe—indeed, as truth itself. This difficulty, manifesting itself in the deeper strata of doubt, by which, at all times, certain intellectually sensitive men have been affected, develops easily into a mental epidemic in epochs in which a certain model of reality crumbles and collapses. It seems that we have lived in such an epoch for a long time. One of its main characteristics has been the uncertainty, steadily increasing in the minds and feelings of men, about the relation between mundane and transcendental reality, or, in other words, about the meaning of life and death, the destiny of the soul, the nature and sanction of moral laws, and the relative domains of knowledge and faith. Insofar as Christianity was the representative religion of the Middle Ages, their model of reality was essentially sacramental. A definite correspondence prevailed between the mundane and transcendental spheres. Faith was not established in any distinct "religious experience," nor as a particular "mode of comprehension," kept apart from "knowledge." It was an element in *all* experience, indeed its crystallizing principle. Only within a mould and pattern determined by faith did experiences make sense and impressions turn to knowledge. This correspondence between the two spheres was so close that at every important stage of a man's life they met and became one in the sacraments.

The sacramental model of reality, intermittently disputed and questioned throughout the whole development of Christian theological thought, was upset in an historically decisive fashion at the time of the Reformation. During that period an intellectual tension, inherent in Christian dogma, developed into a conflagration of vast historical consequences. It produced an articulate climax—which was, however, a mere symptom of a more inarticulate, yet more comprehensive process—at a particularly exposed point of dogmatic faction: the sacramental dispute between Luther and Zwingli. Luther, despite his divergent interpretation of the traditional dogma, represents in it the essentially medieval view, whereas Zwingli, disciple of the humanist Pico della Mirandola, is the spokesman of modernity. To Luther the sacrament of the Last Supper is Christ (the bread and the wine *are* what they represent), while Zwingli reduces it to the status of an allegory (as merely representing what, in itself, it is not). From then onwards the word "merely" has been attaching itself ever more firmly to the word "symbol," soon gaining sufficient strength to bring about a complete estrangement between the two spheres. Finally a new order of things emerged. Within it the transcendental realm is allotted the highest honours of the spirit, but, at the same time, skilfully deprived of a considerable measure of reality; the mundane, on the other hand, is recompensed for its lowering in spiritual stature by the chance of absorbing all available reality and becoming more "really" real than before.

The sudden efflorescence of physical science in the seventeenth century is the positive result of this severance. Its successes have further contributed to the "lower realm" setting itself up as the only "really" real one, and as the sole provider of relevant truth, order and lawfulness. Scientific and other positivist pursuits owe the unchallenged dominion which they have wielded ever since over the intellectual life of Europe to the ever more exclusive fascination which the new model of reality has had for the European mind.

As an unavoidable corollary of this state of affairs, religion and art lost their unquestioned birthright in the homeland of human reality, and turned into strange messengers from the higher unreality, admitted now and then as edifying or entertaining songsters at the positivist banquet. What had once been a matter-of-fact expression of life became a "problem," worthy of a great deal of intellectual fuss and a negligible assignment of reality. As far as the arts are concerned, it is most revealing that the only *distinctive* artistic achievement of Europe since the end of the seventeenth century was accomplished by the art with the least claim to "reality": music, while the most "real" of all arts, architecture, degenerated more and more until it gained new vitality as the unashamed functional servant of technology.

In Germany, a country which, for historical reasons too complex ever to be unravelled, suddenly rose in the eighteenth century, without any gradual transition from the Middle Ages, to the heights of European consciousness and to the fulfilment of the most extravagant intellectual aspirations, the plight of the poet within the new model of reality is most conspicuous. The artist as an exile from reality—this is one of the most authentic themes of German literature, from Goethe's *Tasso* and Grillparzer's *Sappho* to Thomas Mann's *Tonio Kröger*. Kleist, Hölderlin, Nietzsche are the greatest among the victims of a hopeless collision between, on the one hand, the demand for a realization of the spirit within the reality of the world and, on the other, the inexorable resistance of a safely established spirit-proof view of life. Hölderlin is the greatest poet among these involuntary desperadoes of the spirit. His work is one continuous attempt to recapture the lost reality of the symbol and the sacramental experience of life. And for Goethe, to preserve his life, exposed at every point to the revengeful blows of the banished spirit, was, from beginning to end, a struggle, entailing the most precarious manoeuvres of compromise, irony and resignation. It was only— ironically enough—in his scientific activities that he gave vent to his unrestrained fury against the analytical-positivist view of the world and its scientific exposition through mathematics and Newtonian physics. How gloriously he blundered into physical science, determined to meet the enemy on his own ground, and how stubbornly convinced he was of being right! He once said to Eckermann (February 19, 1829):

> Whatever I have achieved as a poet is nothing to be particularly proud of. Excellent poets are my contemporaries, still better poets lived before me, and others will come after me. But in my own country I am the only man who knows what is right in the difficult science of colours; and this is something that gives me real satisfaction and a feeling of superiority over many.

His own idea of science was based upon the *Urphänomen,* a striking assertion of the symbol as the final and irreducible truth of reality.

Goethe lost the battle for the symbol. In the century that stretches between his death and Kafka's writing, reality has been all but completely sealed off against any transcendental intrusion. But in Kafka's work the symbolic substance, forced back in every attempt to attack from above, invades reality from down below, carrying with it the stuff from Hell. Or it need not even invade: Kafka writes at the point where the world, having become too heavy with spiritual emptiness, begins to sink into the unsuspected demon-ridden depths of unbelief. In this cataclysm, the more disastrous because it overtakes a world which has not even believed in its own unbelief, Kafka's heroes struggle in vain for spiritual survival. Thus his creations are symbolic, for they are infused with and not merely allegorical of negative transcendence.

Kafka knew the symbolic or parabolic nature of his work; he knew, too, of the complete alienation of modern man from the reality of the symbol. The following is one of his profoundest meditations. It is called "On Parables" (included in *The Complete Stories*). The German is *"Gleichnisse"* and "symbols" would have been—in this case—a translation equally fitting:

> Many complain that the words of the wise are always merely parables and of no use in daily life, which is the only life we have. When the wise man says: "Go over," he does not mean that we should cross to some actual place, which we could do anyhow if the labour were worth it; he means some fabulous yonder, something unknown to us, something that he too cannot designate more precisely either, and therefore help us here in the very least. All these

parables really set out to say merely that the incomprehensible is incomprehensible, and we know that already. But the cares we have to struggle with every day: that is a different matter.

Concerning this a man once said: Why such reluctance? If you only followed the parables you yourselves would become parables and with that rid of all your daily cares.

Another said: I bet this is also a parable.

The first said: You have won.

The second said: But unfortunately only in parable.

The first said: No, in reality; in parable you have lost.

III

There are, however, allegorical elements to be found in *The Castle:* for instance, the names of many of the characters. The hero himself, who is introduced with the bare initial K. (undoubtedly once again an autobiographical hint—the novel was originally drafted in the first person—and at the same time, through its very incompleteness, suggesting an unrealized, almost anonymous personality) is a land-surveyor. Kafka's choice of this profession for his hero has clearly a meaning. The German for it is *Landvermesser,* and its verbal associations are manifold. The first is, of course, the land-surveyor's professional activity, consisting precisely in what K. desperately desires and never achieves: to produce a workable order within clearly defined boundaries and limits of earthly life, and to find an acceptable compromise between conflicting claims of possession. But *Vermesser* also alludes to *Vermessenheit,* hubris; to the adjective *vermessen,* audacious; to the verb *sich vermessen,* commit an act of spiritual pride, *and* also apply the wrong measure, make a mistake in measurement. The most powerful official of the Castle (for K. the highest representative of authority) is called *Klamm,* a sound producing a sense of anxiety amounting almost to claustrophobia, suggesting straits, pincers, chains, clamps, but also a person's oppressive silence. The messenger of the Castle (as it turns out later, self-appointed and officially never recognized) has the name of *Barnabas,* the same as that man of Cyprus who, though not one of the Twelve, came to rank as an apostle; "Son of Consolation," or "Son of Exhortation," is the biblical meaning of his name, and it is said of him that his exhortation was of the inspiring kind, and so built up faith. And the Barnabas of the novel is indeed a son of consolation, if only in the desperately ironical sense that his family, whom the curse of the Castle has cast into the lowest depths of misery and wretchedness, in vain expects deliverance through his voluntary service for the authority. To K., however, his messages, in all their obscurity and pointlessness, seem the only real link with the Castle, an elusive glimmer of hope, a will-o'-the-wisp of faith. Barnabas's counterpart is *Momus,* the village secretary of Klamm and namesake of that depressing creature, the son of Night, whom the Greek gods authorized to find fault with all things. In the novel it is he whose very existence seems the denial of any hope which Barnabas may have roused in K. *Frieda* (peace) is the girl through whose love K. seeks to reach the goal of his striving; *Bürgel* (diminutive of *Bürge,* guarantor) the name of the little official who offers the solution without K.'s even noticing the chance; and the secretary, through whom K. does expect to achieve something and achieves nothing, is called *Erlanger* (citizen of the town of Erlangen, but also suggestive of *erlangen,* attain, achieve).

This discussion of names provides an almost complete synopsis of the slender plot of *The Castle.* Someone, a man whose name begins with K., and of whom we know no more, neither whence he comes nor what his past life has been, arrives in a village which is ruled by a Castle. He believes that he has been appointed land-surveyor by the authorities. The few indirect contacts that K. succeeds in establishing with the Castle—a letter he receives, a telephone conversation he overhears, yet another letter, and above all the fact that he is joined by two assistants whom the rulers have assigned to him—*seem* to confirm his appointment. Yet he himself is never quite convinced, and never relaxes in his efforts to make sure of it. He feels he must penetrate to the very centre of authority and wring from it a kind of ultra-final confirmation of his claim. Until then he yields, in paralyzed despair, broken by only momentary outbursts of rebellious pride, to the inarticulate, yet absolutely self-assured refusal of the village to acknowledge him as their land-surveyor: "You've been taken on as Land Surveyor, as you say, but, unfortunately, we have no need of a Land Surveyor. There wouldn't be the least use for one here. The frontiers of our little estates are marked out and all officially recorded. So what should we do with a Land Surveyor?" (chap. 5) says the village representative to him.

K.'s belief appears, from the very outset, to be based both on truth and illusion. It is Kafka's all but unbelievable achievement to force, indeed to frighten, the reader into unquestioning acceptance of this paradox, presented with ruthless realism and irresistible logic. Truth and illusion are mingled in K.'s belief in such a way that he is deprived of all order of reality. Truth is permanently on the point of taking off its mask and revealing itself as illusion, illusion in constant danger of being verified as truth. It is the predicament of a man who, endowed with an insatiable appetite for the absolute certainty that transcends all half-truths, relativities and compromises of everyday life, finds himself in a world robbed of all spiritual possessions. Thus he cannot accept the world—the village—without first attaining to that certainty, and he cannot be certain without first accepting the world. Yet every contact with the world makes a mockery of his search, and the continuance of his search turns the world into a mere encumbrance. After studying the first letter from the Castle, K. contemplates his dilemma, "whether he preferred to become a village worker with a distinctive but merely apparent connection with the Castle, or an ostensible village worker whose real occupation was determined through the medium of Barnabas" (chap. 1). From the angle of the village all K.'s contacts with the Castle are figments of his imagination: "You haven't once up till now come into real contact with our authorities. All those contacts have been illusory, but owing to your ignorance of the circumstances you take them to be real" (chap. 5). The Castle, on the other hand, seems to take no notice whatever of the reality of K.'s miserable village existence. In the midst of his suffering the indignity of being employed as a kind of footman to the schoolmaster, and never having come anywhere near working as a land-surveyor, he receives the following letter from Klamm: "The surveying work which you have carried out thus far has been appreciated by me. . . . Do not slacken in your efforts! Carry your work to a fortunate conclusion. Any interruption would displease me. . . . I shall not forget you" (chap. 10). From all this it would appear that it is, in fact, the village that disobeys the will of the Castle, while defeating K. with the powerful suggestion that he misunderstands the intentions of author-ity. And yet the authority seems to give its blessing to the defiance of the village, and to punish K. for his determination to act in accordance with the letter of its orders. In his fanatical obedience it is really he who rebels against the Castle, whereas the village, in its matter-of-fact refusal, lives the life of the Law.

Kafka represents the absolute reversal of German idealism. If it is Hegel's final belief that in the Absolute truth and existence are one, for Kafka it is precisely through the Absolute that they are for ever divided. Truth and existence are mutually exclusive. From his early days onwards it was the keenest wish of Kafka the artist to convey this in works of art; to write in such a way that life, in all its deceptively convincing reality, would be seen as a dream and a nothing before the Absolute:

> Somewhat as if one were to hammer together a table with painful and methodical technical efficiency, and simultaneously do nothing at all, and not in such a way that people could say: "Hammering a table together is nothing to him," but rather "Hammering a table together is really hammering a table together to him, but at the same time it is nothing," whereby certainly the hammering would have become still bolder, still surer, still more real and, if you will, still more senseless.

This is how Kafka, in the series of aphorisms "He" (*The Great Wall of China*), describes the vision of artistic accomplishment which hovered before his mind's eye when, as a young man, he sat one day on the slopes of the Laurenziberg in Prague. Has he, in his later works, achieved this artistic justification of nonentity? Not quite; what was meant to become the lifting of a curse through art, became the artistically perfect realization of it, and what he dreamed of making into something as light as a dream, fell from his hand with the heaviness of a nightmare. Instead of a vindication of nothingness, he achieved the portrayal of the most cunningly vindictive unreality.

It is hard to understand how *The Castle* could possibly be called a religious allegory with a pilgrim of the type of Bunyan's as its hero. Pilgrimage? On the contrary, the most oppressive quality of Kafka's work is the unshakable stability of its central situation. It takes place in a world that knows of no motion, no change, no metamorphosis— unless it be the transformation of a human being into an insect. Its caterpillars never turn into butterflies, and when the leaves of a tree tremble it is not due to the wind: it is the stirring of a serpent coiled round its branches. Pilgrim or not, there is no progress to be watched in *The Castle,* unless we agree to call progress what Kafka describes in "A Little Fable" (*The Complete Stories*) as the "progress" of the mouse:

> "Alas," said the mouse, "the world is growing smaller every day. At the beginning it was so big that I was afraid, I kept running and running, and I was glad when at last I saw walls far away to the right and left, but these long walls have narrowed so quickly that I am in the last chamber already, and there in the corner stands the trap that I must run into." "You only need to change your direction," said the cat, and ate it up.

It was been said that Kafka has this in common with Bunyan, "that the goal and the road indubitably exist, and that the necessity to find them is urgent." Only the second point is correct. Indeed, so urgent is it for Kafka to discover the road and reach the goal that life seems impossible without this achievement. But do road and goal exist? "There is a goal, but no way; what we call the way is only wavering," is what Kafka says about it in "Reflections on Sin. . . ." And is there really a goal for him? This is the answer that Kafka gives to himself in "He":

> He feels imprisoned on this earth, he feel constricted: the melancholy, the impotence, the sickness, the feverish fancies of the captive afflict him; no comfort can comfort him, since it is merely comfort, gentle head-splitting comfort glozing the brutal fact of imprisonment. But if he is asked what he actually wants he cannot reply, for—that is one of his strongest proofs—he has no conception of freedom.

Kafka's hero is the man who *believes* in absolute freedom but cannot have any conception of it because he *exists* in a world of slavery. Therefore it is not grace and salvation that he seeks, but either his right or—a bargain with the powers. "I don't want any act of favour from the Castle, but my rights" (chap. 5), says K. in his interview with the village representative. But convinced of the futility of this expectation, his real hope is based on Frieda, his fiancée and Klamm's former mistress, whom he is obviously prepared to hand back to him "for a price."

In K.'s relationship to Frieda the European story of romantic love has found its epilogue. It is the solid residue left behind by the evaporated perfume of romance, revealing its darkest secret. In romantic love, as it has dominated a vast section of European literature ever since the later Middle Ages, individualism, emerging from the ruins of a common spiritual order, has found its most powerful means of transcendence. The spiritually more and more autonomous, and therefore more and more lonely, individual worships Eros, and his twin deity within the romantic imagination: Death, as the only gods capable of breaking down the barriers of his individualist isolation. Therefore love becomes tragedy: overcharged with unmanageable spiritual demands it must needs surge ahead of any human relationship. In its purest manifestations, romantic love is a glorious disaster of the soul, carrying frustration in its wake. For what the romantic lover seeks is not really the beloved. Intermixed with his erotic craving, inarticulate, diffuse, and yet dominating it, is the desire for spiritual salvation. Even a "happy ending" spells profound disillusionment for the romantic expectation. Perhaps it is Strindberg, deeply admired by Kafka, who wrote the last chapter of its history. It is certainly Kafka who wrote its postscript.

For K. loves Frieda—if he loves her at all—entirely for Klamm's sake. This is not only implied in the whole story of K. and Frieda, but explicitly stated by Kafka in several passages which he later deleted, very probably because their directness seemed to him incompatible with the muted meaning of the book. As an indictment of K., it is contained in the protocol about his life in the village which Momus has drawn up, and in which K. is accused of having made up to Frieda out of a "calculation of the lowest sort": because he believed that in her he would win a mistress of Klamm's and so possess "a pledge for which he can demand the highest price." On the margin of the protocol there was also "a childishly scrawled drawing, a man with a girl in his arms. The girl's face was buried in the man's chest, but the man who was much the taller, was looking over the girl's shoulders at a sheet of paper he had in his hands and on which he was joyfully inscribing some figures." But perhaps still more conclusive than Momus's clearly hostile interpretation is another deleted passage giving K.'s own reflections on his love for Frieda:

And then immediately, before there was any time to think, Frieda had come, and with her the belief, which it was impossible to give up entirely even today, that through her mediation an almost physical relationship to Klamm, a relationship so close that it amounted almost to a whisper-ing form of communication, had come about, of which for the present only K. knew, which however needed only a little intervention, a word, a glance, in order to reveal itself primarily to Klamm, but then too to everyone, as some-thing admittedly incredible which was nevertheless, through the compulsion of life, the compulsion of the loving embrace, a matter of course. . . . What was he without Frieda? A nonentity, staggering along after . . . will-o'-the-wisps.

The desperate desire for spiritual certainty is all that is left of romantic love. K. *wills* his love for Frieda because he *wills* his salvation. He is a kind of Pelagius believing that he "can if he ought," yet living in a relentlessly predestined world. This situation produces a theology very much after the model of Gnostic and Manichaean beliefs. The incarnation is implicitly denied in an unmitigated loathing of "deter-mined" matter, and the powers which rule are perpetually suspected of an alliance with the Devil because they have consented to the creation of such a loathsome world. Heaven is at least at seven removes from the earth, and only begins where no more neighbourly relations are possible. There are no real points of contact between divinity and the earth, which is not even touched by divine emanation. Reality is the sovereign domain of strangely unangelic angels, made up of evil and hostility. The tedious task of the soul is, with much wisdom of initiation and often with cunning diplomacy, gradually to by-pass the armies of angels and the strong-points of evil, and finally to slip into the remote kingdom of light.

The Castle of Kafka's novel is, as it were, the heavily fortified garrison of a company of Gnostic demons, successfully holding an advanced position against the manoeuvres of an impatient soul. There is no conceivable idea of divinity which could justify those interpreters who see in the Castle the residence of "divine law and divine grace." Its officers are totally indifferent to good if they are not positively wicked. Neither in their decrees nor in their activities is there any trace of love, mercy, charity, or majesty. In their icy detachment they inspire certainly no awe, but fear and revulsion. Their servants are a plague to the village, "a wild, unmanageable lot, ruled by their insatiable impulses . . . their scandalous behaviour knows no limits" (chap. 15), an anticipation of the blackguards who were to become the footmen of European dictators rather than the office-boys of a divine ministry. Compared to the petty and apparently calculated torture of this tyranny, the gods of Shakespeare's indignation who "kill us for their sport" are at least majestic in their wantonness.

From the very beginning there is an air of indecency, indeed of obscenity, about the inscrutable rule of the castle. A newcomer in the village, K. meets the teacher in the company of children. He asks him whether he knows the Count and is surprised at the negative answer: " 'What, you don't know the Count?' 'Why should I?' replied the teacher in a low tone, and added aloud in French: 'Please remember that there are innocent children present' " (chap. 1). And, indeed, what an abhorrent rule it is! The souls of women seem to be allowed to enter the next realm if they surrender, as a sort of pass, their bodies to the officials. They are then married off to some nincompoop in the village, with their drab existence rewarded only by occasional flashes of voluptuously blissful memories of their sacrificial sins. Damnation is their lot if they refuse, as happens in the case of Amalia, Barnabas's sister, who brought degradation upon herself and her family by declining the invitation of the official Sortini.

No, the Castle does not represent, as some early interpreters believed, divine guidance or even Heaven itself. It is for K. something that is to be conquered, something that bars his way into a purer realm. K.'s antagonism to the Castle becomes clear from the very first pages of the book. This is how he responds to the first telephone conversation about his appointment which, in his presence, is conducted between the village and the authorities:

> K. pricked up his ears. So the Castle had recognized him as the Land Surveyor. That was unpropitious for him, on the one hand, for it meant that the Castle was well informed about him, had estimated all the probable chances and was taking up the challenge with a smile. On the other hand, however, it was quite propitious, for if his interpretation was right, they had underestimated his strength, and he would have more freedom of action than he had dared to hope.
>
> (chap. 1)

The correspondence between the spiritual structure of *The Castle* and the view of the world systematized into Gnostic and Manichaean dogma is indeed striking. There is, however, no reason to assume that Kafka had thoroughly studied those ancient heresies. In their radical dualism they are merely the model systems of a deep-rooted spiritual disposition, asserting itself over and over again in individuals and whole movements. Gnostic and Manichaean is, above all "the face that is filled with loathing and hate" at the sight of physical reality. Kafka refrains from any dealings with nature, such as are found, for instance, in his earliest story *Description of a Struggle*. There is, apart from the mention of a starry sky, wind and snow, not one description of nature in *The Castle*. Within the human sphere everything that is of the flesh is treated with a sense of nausea and disgust. All the habitations of men are lightless, airless and dirty. The nuptial embrace between K. and Frieda takes place amidst puddles of beer on the floor of a public bar, the room still filled with the stale smells of an evening's business, while mass prostitution is carried on in the stable of the inn.

But Kafka has also found subtler means of conveying his revolt against "matter." One evening K. is waiting in the dark courtyard of the inn for Klamm to emerge from his village room and enter his sledge. The coachman, noticing K., encourages him to wait inside the sledge and have a drink from one of the bottles kept in the sidepockets. K. opens the bottle and smells:

> Involuntarily he smiled, the perfume was so sweet, so caressing, like praise and good words from someone whom one loves very much yet one does not know clearly what they are for and has no desire to know, and is simply happy in the knowledge that it is one's friend who is saying them. "Can this be brandy?" K. asked him doubtfully and took a taste out of curiosity. Yes, strangely enough it was brandy, and burned and warmed. How strangely it was transformed in drinking out of something which seemed hardly more than a sweet perfume into a drink fit for a coachman!
>
> (chap. 8)

Whether intentional or not, this profanation of the aroma of a spirit in the process of its being "realized" is a wonderfully subtle symbol of a Manichaean perspective of the world.

The Castle is, no doubt, the highest realm K. is capable of perceiving. This is what misled the critics, but not Kafka himself, into equating it with God. But it is certainly not quite irrelevant that in his personal confessions Kafka hardly ever utters the belief that the incessant striving of his spirit was directed towards God, or prompted by *amor Dei*. Almost all the time his soul is preoccupied with the power of Evil; a power so great that God had to retreat before it into purest transcendence, for ever out of reach of life. Thus the idea of final authority, merely by assuming the shape of physical reality in *The Castle,* falls, without the author's either willing it or being able to help it, under the spell of Evil. It is the paradox of spiritual absolutism that the slightest touch of concreteness will poison the purest substance of the spirit, and one ray of darkness blot out a world of light.

Although seemingly quantitative assessments of this kind are always problematical, it is true to say that *The Castle* is even more "Manichaean" than *The Trial*. Yet even here it sometimes, if rarely, seems that the sinister threat to the spirit, embodied in a senseless world, might suddenly reveal itself as a disguised promise of happiness, a happiness and even goodness born of the non-resistance to that world, indeed its resolute acceptance: "you must take the side of the world." Although the cursed rule of the castle is the furthest point of the world to which this wakeful mind can reach, there dawns, at its extreme boundaries, a light, half suspectingly perceived, half stubbornly ignored, that comes from things outside the scope of Klamm's authority. K. is possessed by only one thought: that he must come to grips with Klamm; yet at the same time he knows that his very obsession with this thought precludes him from reaching what he mistakenly believes only Klamm can give. He senses that, if only he could renounce his consuming desire, he would find what eludes him because of his very striving for it. In Pepi who, for a short time, was promoted to the rank of barmaid in the local inn, and thus enjoys the honour of serving beer to Klamm, K. meets the carica-tured personification of his own ambition. In giving advice to her he shows a remarkable knowledge of his own malady:

> It is a job like any other, but for you it is heaven, consequently you set about everything with exaggerated eagerness, . . . tremble for the job, feel you are constantly being persecuted, try by means of being excessively

pleasant to win over everyone who in your opinion might be a support to you, but in this way bother them and repel them, for what they want at the inn is peace and quiet and not the barmaid's worries on top of their own.

And later:

When I compare myself with you . . . , it is as if we had both striven too intensely, too noisily, too childishly, with too little experience, to get something that for instance with Frieda's calm and Frieda's matter-of-factness can be got easily and without much ado. We have tried to get it by crying, by scratching, by tugging—just as a child tugs at the tablecloth, gaining nothing, but only bringing all the splendid things down on the floor and putting them out of reach for ever.

(chap. 20)

But it is in K.'s adventure with the Castle official Bürgel that this insight finds its most striking expression. K., summoned in the middle of the night to an interview with the official Erlanger, has, in his weariness and exhaustion, forgotten the number of the door, and enters, more in the sleepy hope of finding an empty bed there than an official of the Castle, another room. There he encounters the official Bürgel. The ensuing dialogue, or monologue rather, is one of Kafka's greatest feats in the art of melting the solid flesh of a grotesque reality and revealing behind it the anatomy of the miraculous. Bürgel promises K. to settle once and for all his affair in the Castle. K. is not in the least impressed by this offer. He waves it aside as the boast of a dilettante:

Without knowing anything of the circumstances under which K.'s appointment had come about, the difficulties that it encountered in the community and at the Castle, of the complications that had already occurred during K.'s sojourn here or had been foreshadowed, without knowing anything of all this, indeed without even showing, what should have been expected of a secretary, that he had at least an inkling of it all, he offered to settle the whole *affaire* up there in no time at all with the aid of his little note-pad.

It is the unbelief of a labyrinthine mind in the very existence of simplicity. And while K. grows ever more weary, Bürgel delivers, in a rapturous crescendo, the message of the miracle: If a man takes a secretary of the Castle by surprise; if, in the middle of the night, the applicant, almost unconscious of what he does, slips, like a tiny grain through a perfect sieve, through the network of difficulties that is spread over all approaches to the centre of authority, then the Castle, in the person of this one secretary, must yield to the intruder, indeed must almost force the utterly unexpected granting of his request upon the supplicant: "You think it cannot happen at all? You are right, it cannot happen at all. But some night—for who can vouch for everything?—it *does* happen." It is an event so rare that it seems to occur merely by virtue of rumour, and even if it does occur, one can, as it were, render it innocuous "by proving to it, which is very easy, that there is no room for it in this world" (chap. 18). And Bürgel goes on with his rhapsody, describing the shattering delight with which a secretary responds to this situation. But when he ends, K. is sound asleep, and, with the conditions of the miracle fulfilled before his eyes, as unaware of its possibility as he had been in his tortured wakeful pursuit of it.

Indeed, no comfort can be found *within* this world. Yet the power not only to experience but poetically to create this world must have its source outside. Only a mind keeping alive in at least one of its recesses the memory of a place where the soul is truly at home is able to contemplate with such creative vigour the struggles of a man lost in a hostile land; and only an immensity of goodness can be so helplessly overcome by the vision of the worst of all possible worlds. This is the reason why we are not merely terrified by the despair of this book, but also moved by its sadness, the melancholy of spiritual failure carrying with it a hardly perceptible faith, the very faith of which all but inexhaustible resources are needed, as Kafka believed, for merely carrying on the business of every day.

In one of his most Manichaean sayings—in "Reflections on Sin, . . ."—Kafka speaks of the power of a single crow to destroy the heavens; but, he adds, this "proves nothing against the heavens for the heavens signify simply: The impossibility of crows." And although these birds swarm ceaselessy around the Castle, its builder built it from the impulse to render them impossible. Is it, one wonders, yet another phantom hope in a deluded world that prompts in the book a child, a simple girl and a wretched family to turn with a mysteriously messianic expectation to the land-surveyor K.? And makes, in one version of Kafka's attempt to continue the unfinished manuscript, an old woman say of the homeless stranger: "This man shouldn't be let go to the dogs." Or is it perhaps the reflection of a faith, maintained even in the grip of damnation, a faith which Nietzsche once expressed: "Whosoever has built a new Heaven, has found the strength for it only in his own Hell" (chap. 15)?

Power and Authority
in *The Castle*

Richard J. Arneson

Franz Kafka's enigmatic novel, *The Castle,* has seemed a religious parable to many commentators. The meaning of this parable is a matter of dispute. One view has it that Kafka's attitude is akin to that of the philosopher of religion, Søren Kierkegaard: religious faith is counterposed to secular reason, and the presence of genuine faith is marked by a willingness to transcend secular ethical concerns, to do what (from a human standpoint) appears unreasonable or even evil because it is God's command. Taking its cue from the fact that the novel's protagonist, the land-surveyor K., fails to gain from the authority figures he beseeches any rational explanation of the morally troubling features of his case, this Kierkegaardian interpretation suggests that perhaps the point of the novel is that K. sins by insisting on rational explanation. K.'s failure is his grudging refusal to make the "teleological suspension of the ethical" recommended by Kierkegaard and urged by several characters within the novel.

Some have felt uneasy with a reading of the novel which by its implicit identification of Kafka's castle with the Judeo-Christian God renders an adverse judgment on K. in his conflict with the Castle authorities. Of course it is possible to accept the identification and yet reverse the judgment. A second view does just this by substituting Friedrich Nietzsche in the place of Søren Kierkegaard and registering the differences between these two philosophers in its

From *Mosaic* 12, no. 4 (Summer 1979). © 1979 by the University of Manitoba Press. All translations of *Das Schloss* are by Willa and Edwin Muir.

decoding of *The Castle*'s message. If this is a religious novel, the argument runs, then the theme is the death of God. K. is a man who lives in an age when the idea of God and more generally of absolute ethical values is in a state of decay, no longer capable of commanding assent. Hence the deity is symbolized by a ramshackle, decomposing Castle, one whose very existence is problematic. The fictional world of *The Castle* is godless, but filled with people who retain a deep longing for the divine and for the security a divinely-ordained (or otherwise certain) ethics promises. These old absolutes are no longer available, if ever they were, but we humans have not yet adjusted to this state of affairs. *The Castle* becomes on this reading a post-Christian novel, with its characters seen as living out various unsatisfactory solutions to the problem of religious faith. The villagers cling to the old faith at all costs, and there is something sinister in their willful naïveté. On the other hand, K.'s problem is that he insists on seeking satisfaction where there is plainly no satisfaction to be had. There is no God to answer his demands; there is no timeless ethical framework waiting to be discovered through his searches. If God is dead, one ought not to continue to serve him as the villagers desperately try to do. But if God is dead, asking him to please ratify one's title as land-surveyor is equally inappropriate.

The tendency of a Nietzschean interpretation is excessively to belittle K.'s aggressive striving against the Castle. I believe that a concern to correct this tendency is part of what has motivated commentators to elaborate a third religious interpretation of Kafka's parable from the standpoint of a secular humanism. Suppose we identify Kafka's authorial point-of-view on the novel with that of its central character, K., who then becomes a straightforward hero of the story, which will now be seen as recording his stubborn and overwhelmingly admirable resistance to a moral wrong perpetrated against him by the constituted authority of the Castle. The novel asserts the claims of moral autonomy and ethical rationality against the ominous ideal of submitting to an inscrutable divine will for man. If God's ways are really inscrutable as they are in the world of *The Castle,* then those ways are irrelevant to human morality. From this standpoint, the most salient fact about K. is that he makes a simple and unambiguous moral claim against the Castle authorities, and never gives it up despite the villagers' recommendations. He insists on his rights in the face of the Castle's apparent disregard of them.

In so doing he calls to mind John Stuart Mill's statement that he would not worship an evil God or do evil deeds on his command, even if the consequence should be that this evil God would punish him for an eternity in hell. The nuantial difference between Kafka and Mill—which explains why the larger affinity is often missed—is that Kafka is more aware of the uncertainties and ambiguities of the moral life: we can never have certain evidence for the rightness of our chosen course, and must do the best we can despite this nagging lack of assurance. In contrast to the death-of-God interpretation, the Mill interpretation does not insist that an objectively valid ethics is impossible of attainment, but rather holds that, if it be attainable, it can be gained only through rational inquiry and not through religious or pseudo-religious abandonment of reason. We can have good reasons for doing what we do, but "authority says so" cannot by itself constitute a good reason. K. refers to this line of thought several times in the novel, but perhaps never so explicitly as when he says to Olga: "Fear of the authorities is born in you here, and is further suggested to you all your lives in the most various ways and from every side, and you yourselves help to strengthen it as much as possible." K. goes on to say that he has no fundamental objection to that, for "if an authority is good, why should it not be feared?" Unlike the villagers, K. distinguishes authority from good authority and insists on independent and compelling evidence for deeming an authority good.

In this [essay] I offer a rather literal-minded political interpretation of Franz Kafka's novel, which is yet capable of accommodating the undeniable presence in the novel of the themes that have elicited religious interpretations. No doubt the attitude of the villagers toward the Castle above them is very much akin to religious faith, but as the protagonist of the story remarks, theirs is a "reverence that dishonors its object." *The Castle* describes a world in which political relations are suffused with religious veneration. The villagers act toward their political rulers, the Castle officials, as it would be appropriate to behave toward a genuinely religious authority. The outsider who insistently demands that the Castle ratify his disputed title as land-surveyor, K. questions this predominant village attitude; so far the reader's sympathies are with him. However, K. shares with the villagers a nest of attitudes concerning power, status, and hierarchy, so that his rejection of village folkways is very far from unequivocal. Kafka's achievement is to have depicted K. on the one hand as grasping, snobbish, and vulgarly ambitious, on the other hand as expressing in the thrust of his life a valid moral censure of the Castle, and to have done this in such a way that the two depictions fit together credibly in a single character.

In what follows I try to show how K.'s stature as a flawed hero casts a dark shadow on interpretations of the novel that conflate the distinct issues, whether K.'s moral criticism of the Castle is justified, and whether K. possesses the sort of character capable of pressing his critique of the Castle through to a successful resolution. Our insight into K.'s character develops largely by way of reflection on the political and social milieu against which his personality is delineated. What emerges from this is a reading of the novel which sees in it a commentary on the pseudo-religiosity manifest in the treatment the villagers accord to the feudal-bureaucratic enigma that rules them, as well as a gentle but forceful commentary on the romantic individualist rebellion carried out by K. against the cult of veneration surrounding the Castle.

The village is entirely subservient to the distant Castle: the villagers bow down before its authority and they do so with a considered appreciation of just how much deference is owed to each personage. The novel is replete with scenes of characters fencing about with one another to determine who ranks higher in the status hierarchy. When village characters voice their aspirations to higher status—and every important character does this, with the single exception of Amalia—they do so in tones appropriate to the confiding of their deepest values. The world of the Castle is an elaborate pecking order, in which everybody is acutely conscious of status and seeks to maintain a sense of self-respect through his awareness that some persons rank lower in the scheme of social estimation, and through participation in social courtesies reinforcing this sensitivity to caste gradations. (The term "caste" here may be misleading, as tending to imply the presence of social distinctions rigidly fixed by birth. In the world of this novel there is some limited social mobility, both upward and downward, so there is some basis for feeling personally responsible for one's social position.) What is perhaps most noteworthy about K. is that he is as caught up as any villager in the project of ratifying self-worth through the gratifications of hierarchical status. In the last resort what he seeks is a higher place in the pecking order. Towards this end his relations with the villagers he encounters tend to be instrumental and manipulative in character.

It is true that there is more to K. than the social-climbing dimension of his personality. At least two sides of K. are revealed in his assault on the Castle. One, especially apparent in the early chapters of the novel, is his rasping ambition; the other, plainly exhibited in the interview with the village elder and intermittently visible throughout the story, is his idealistic willingness to call to account authority figures who fail to meet common-sense moral standards. To understand K.'s actual role in the novel and in the plan of Kafka's intentions, it is necessary to insist on both aspects of K.'s quest, for he is equally injured plaintiff before the law and fortune-hunter in the shadow of the Castle.

The early chapters pile up an impressive mound of evidence concerning the extent to which K. is implicated in the most unappealing features of the village outlook. For example, K. is snobbish in his initial meeting with the family of Barnabas the messenger. K. had taken a walk with Barnabas in the hope of arriving at the Castle leaning on the arm of this man who seemed to have influential connections there. Instead Barnabas takes K. to his family home. The rude surroundings convince K. that this man is too low in status to be any help in his attempts to gain a respectful hearing from Castle officials. From that moment K. reacts to this family with open contempt, despite their friendliness. A passage deleted from Kafka's final draft of the novel is very explicit in revealing K.'s motive to be to seek the company of those with high caste standing and to avoid association with those who have no status to confer on him. By contrast, a day earlier K. was struck by the appearance of a woman whose dress shines as though made of silk, an indication that she is from a higher social class than the peasants around her. She confirms this impression in telling K. she is a girl from the Castle. Kafka takes pains to describe this woman as having no attractive qualities apart from the aura of the Castle that lingers about her, but this suffices to attract K. In part K.'s interest in this woman is occasioned by the thought that having been a resident of the Castle, she may be able to help him gain entrance there, but the suggestion is strongly imprinted on this scene that K. is infatuated with this woman and that this infatuation is stimulated largely by her association with the Castle.

K.'s romantic inclinations are bound up with his longing for the Castle. The theme of power and authority is traceable through the presentation of sexual relations in the novel. Power and status, as found in Klamm (who in other respects is a bland cipher), and proximity to power and status, as in Frieda while she is Klamm's mistress, are the key determinants of sexual attractiveness for K. and for others. K.'s shifting attitudes toward Frieda illustrate this obsessive syndrome.

When K. first meets Frieda she is securely established in the roles of Herrenhof barmaid and mistress of Klamm, and what K. first notices about her is her look of conscious superiority. He quickly becomes romantically involved with her. Almost as quickly, as their fortunes plummet, K. becomes disenchanted with Frieda, and among her recriminations against him is the charge that all along he has feigned feelings of affection in order to use her to advance his cause. What seems to have happened is rather that, once removed from the Herrenhof barroom with its suggestion of quasi-official intimacy with Klamm, Frieda no longer holds the attraction for K. that was bound up with that ambience. Looking at his drooping lover amidst their humiliating troubles, K. surmises that it had been the "nearness of Klamm that had made her so irrationally seductive, in that seduction she had drawn K. to him, and now she was withering in his arms."

In his romantic hankerings K. participates in the culture of the village. Other villagers behave similarly. Perhaps the most indelicate instance of a mingling of feelings of love and sexual affection with feelings of class snobbery and deference to power is the life story of Gardena, the Bridge Inn landlady. Peremptorily summoned by Klamm many years ago, she was his lover on three occasions; then abruptly his calls ceased. The memory of this brief and rather pathetic interlude has dominated her life. Her present husband courted her by commiserating with her about Klamm's fickleness; to this day their relation largely consists of his sympathy for her plight as she pines away for Klamm. Gardena avows that as a matter of course she would return to Klamm's bed in the unlikely event that he should call her back. Meanwhile she holds his memory sacred, venerating three keepsakes of the affair as though they were holy relics. Upon hearing this story, K. makes the conventionally appropriate objection to Gardena's obsession and her husband's acceptance of it, but what is interesting is that K. does not press this objection at all forcefully. K.'s identification with Gardena in this matter is sufficiently strong to render perfunctory and almost lackadaisical his championing of her husband's case.

In the same vein, it is instructive to consider Olga's remarkable commentary on the romantic relations between Castle gentlemen and village commoners. Olga rests her negative judgment on her sister Amalia's conduct (of which, more later) on the unusual claim that fundamentally different standards of morality apply to Castle lords and village folk. Norms of reciprocity and mutual respect may perhaps be all very well for marriages within the village, but for affairs involving a Castle gentleman, a different code is binding. The code demands the utmost in self-abnegation from villagers and imposes scarcely any discernible requirements at all on the conduct of those from the Castle. According to this perverse code it is not the official Sortini who commits a transgression by brusquely ordering Amalia to his bed, but Amalia who does wrong in refusing to submit to Sortini's "romantic" demands. The overwhelming impression Olga's tales convey is that while sexual attraction crosses class boundaries (indeed Olga assumes any sexual encounter with any official would be welcome to every village girl), ordinary moral conceptions do not hold across the boundaries of class, with the natural consequence that the authority of ordinary norms of human decency is eroded in relationships among villagers as well.

Besides exhibiting the dialectic of sex and power sketched above, K.'s relationship with Frieda illustrates how K. is both caught up in the village mentality and in some sense morally above it. Frieda is attracted to K. by his disagreeable ambition. In a vague way she understands that K.'s project of gaining satisfaction from a face-to-face confrontation with a high Castle official, if successfully completed, would raise his social status, and with this aspect of K.'s project she fully identifies. So far as I can discern, the episodes of the novel in which Frieda figures give no hint that she has any understanding of the moral dimension of K.'s aggression against the Castle. Frieda exactly corresponds to the stereotyped image of a housewife who is loyally devoted to her husband and prizes the material signs of her husband's achievements, but is unaware of the morally problematic scenarios within which "masculine" striving for achievement occurs. When K. idealizes Frieda it is this—admittedly engaging—caricature of the "feminine" virtues he is praising. K.'s praises reflect his own ambivalence about the morally serious side of his personality which Frieda blithely ignores.

In contrasting the philistine Frieda with the philistine-but-also conscientious K., one assumes there is in K. an element of disinterested moral concern. K.'s initial motivation for approaching the Castle is his desire to see to it that the Castle keeps its end of a bargain struck with him. K. is insisting on his contractual rights. He believes the Castle owes him a clarification of his occupational status and the provision of useful work for him to perform.

In the opening pages of the story K. appears to be casting about for a wider significance to confer on his activity. He offers obscure hints that his project may become part of a broader campaign against the Castle, but as these hints are never developed, they serve mainly to plant a doubt in the reader's mind as to what sort of game K. is really playing. The interview with the village elder or mayor in chapter 5 conclusively dispels this doubt, to my mind, and establishes that the Castle is an oppressive organization against which a man like K. does well to be on his guard. In the course of rehearsing K.'s case the village elder describes Castle officialdom as a convoluted, almost anarchic bureaucracy in which a mad proliferation of paperwork is accompanied by a dreamlike indifference to the human lives that are arbitrarily shuffled about with that paperwork. This is an evilly inefficient operation that one can readily imagine to be capable of hiring a man from afar and ignoring him on his arrival. From the elder's story it seems there isn't anything the Castle officials could conceivably do that would alter the villagers' steady conviction that the Castle represents a legitimate authority over their lives. For once in the novel K. does not acquiesce in the craziness confronting him. His tone of appalled common-sense decency is perfectly apt in the circumstances; more importantly, he sustains this tone through to the conclusion of the interview. The mayor complacently explains that K. is caught in a Catch-22 bind, for since the workings of the Castle bureaucracy are assumed to be perfectly just and error-free there are no procedures for redressing errors that do occur or correcting injustices that are perpetrated. K. remarks that the mayor's story amuses him only in that it "gives me an insight into the ludicrous bungling that in certain circumstances may decide the life of a human being."

The most revealing display of K.'s moral resolution occurs when he waits for Klamm in the snow outside the Herrenhof. Before analyzing this incident it will be necessary to digress, in order to clarify an element in K.'s character not so far mentioned, which figures decisively in the manner of his waiting in this scene. At one point in the narrative the Herrenhof landlady shrewdly observes that

K. is like a small boy. The stress on K.'s childish and childlike qualities calls to mind parent-child conflict as the analogue of K.'s dealings with the Castle, and this analogy tends both to import into K.'s saga the emotional intensity and occasional fierceness of generational conflict and to downgrade the moral issues posed by K.'s challenge to the Castle. To talk about power relations and authority conflicts in terms of parent-child struggles is strongly to suggest the legitimacy of the authority under challenge. Although the tendency of this parent/child imagery is deflationary, this deflation is never complete. Partly this is so because the Castle officials are not described in parental terms so as to complete the analogy. Partly this is so because K. is only intermittently described as a child, while at other points in the narrative his mature understanding is emphasized, particularly in contrast to the genuinely childish characters such as the assistants Arthur and Jeremiah and the chambermaid Pepi.

It is not easy to browse in the novel at any length without coming across passages that show K. behaving childishly. At the beginning of the interview with the village elder, for example, K. "had this sense of extraordinary ease in intercourse with the authorities. They seemed literally to bear every burden, one could lay everything on their shoulders and remain free and untouched oneself." These expectations which K. brings to his negotiation with the village elder are the demands of a child's fantasy. It is no discredit on Castle officials that they fail to meet such infantile expectations as these. Their faults lie elsewhere.

After noting this childishness in K., we are in a position to make sense of the scene at the Herrenhof courtyard, where in one respect K.'s behaviour begs for the indulgent dismissal appropriate to youthful misdemeanor, while in another and more important respect K.'s behaviour demands the serious recognition appropriate to considered adult action. The best and worst of K. are both manifested when he resolves to force an interview with Klamm through the strategem of waiting outside the Herrenhof alongside the carriage that is scheduled to return Klamm to the Castle. The carriage-driver invites K. to take a drink of Klamm's brandy and, as a favor, to pass the brandy back to him. K. clambers into the carriage and loses himself in a childish revel, sniffing the brandy and relaxing on the luxurious furs and pillows that line the carriage interior. K. momentarily forgets the carriage-driver's request for a drink. Suddenly light bathes the courtyard, footsteps draw near, and K. is virtually caught in the act of trespass. As spilled brandy drips down the sideboard, signalling K.'s guilt, K. forms the mean intention to implicate the carriage-driver in his misconduct, should an embarrassing interrogation commence. Instead, what transpires is that a minor official orders K. to leave so as to make way for Klamm's departure. K. refuses to leave, and is left standing alone in the snow. K. then muses to himself:

> It seemed to K. as if at last those people had broken off all relations with him, and as if now in reality he were freer than he had ever been, and at liberty to wait in this place, usually forbidden to him, as long as he desired, and had won a freedom such as hardly anybody else had ever succeeded in winning, and as if nobody could dare to touch him or drive him away, or even speak to him; but—this conviction was at least equally strong—as if at the same time there was nothing more senseless, nothing more hopeless, than this freedom, this waiting, this inviolability.

In this fine passage K. expresses a sense of achievement and a doubt about the value of that achievement. Both feelings are intelligible in the light of the analysis already offered. The autonomy that K. has won in his insistence on waiting for Klamm in the face of a contrary order, is a genuine moral achievement; what is at stake is not so much the Castle's supposed inability to force him to leave the premises as the discovery that the Castle cannot coerce his conscientious choice. However, this moral freedom, as K. experiences it, is bound up with isolation, an isolation moreover that is not linked by any necessity to K.'s conscientious refusal. K. has brought the isolation on himself in this instance by his childishly self-centered unkindness to the carriage-driver, and more generally by his scrambling, hustling life outlook.

K.'s sense of inadequacy in the scene by the carriage arises from his inchoate belief that community matters, and that the absence of community from his life is a matter for which he is in some way personally responsible. The recognition that K. desperately seeks from the Castle is to be had only in the village. This recognition, however, is not to be found through immersion in the traditional village community, with its obeisance to Castle ways, but through building a new community in the village founded on a common policy of insisting on villagers' rights against Castle authority. Kafka does not say this. What he does do is show, with subtle urgency, a variety of debacles in which other possible life-strategies eventuate— K.'s, Frieda's, Gardena's, Amalia's, Olga's, Barnabas's, the village elder's, Pepi's, the assistants', and so on. A process of elimination tentatively leads the reader's mind to an affirmation beyond the doubting tone of the novel. The nature of this affirmation will perhaps become clearer after considering the two most attractive life-strategies paired against one another.

In their own ways both K. and Amalia have offered high-minded resistance to overbearing Castle authority, and thus are kindred spirits. It is initially puzzling that when they meet in the course of the novel they have virtually nothing to say to each other. K. hears the story of Amalia's resolute defiance of the Castle's petty malice from her sister Olga, who is not disposed to be generous in her opinion of Amalia, but who nonetheless tells a story that, one would suppose, cannot fail to elicit K.'s admiration. The story is that a high Castle official, Sortini, having observed Amalia at a village Fire Brigade Festival, next morning sent her a vulgar message commanding that she come to him and, apparently, gratify his lust for her. Amalia tears up the message in a rage, and when word of her defiance spreads around the village, all the villagers ostracize the family. Amalia tends her ailing parents, who break down under the strain of this ostracism, while Olga carries out the obscure project of atoning for the family's "sin" by humbling herself before the Castle officials' servants, sleeping with any who will have her.

As often, K.'s initial response is adequate ("surely Amalia couldn't be accused or punished because of Sortini's criminal actions?") but this response evaporates in a mist of second thoughts. In the end K. insists to Olga that he finds Amalia morally unattractive and Olga herself very fetching. K.'s preference is disconcerting, but Amalia appears to have formed as unfavorable an impression of K. as K. entertains of her. She teases K. mercilessly about his selfish ambition, and to these taunts he rejoins with gibes against her self-willed isolation. Both K. and Amalia seem to be scoring reasonable points in these exchanges.

My view is that Kafka uses each of these characters as a foil to set off the distinctive qualities of the other, so that on the one hand Amalia is rightly disgusted by K.'s wheeling and dealing and on the other hand K. is justly suspicious of Amalia's arrogance and contempt for all villagers who have not yet adopted the principled stance against the Castle which she has taken. K. does not appreciate Amalia's disinterestedness and purity of heart, but then Amalia does not appreciate K.'s gregariousness and organizing ambition. Since it is understandable that people typically do not seek out their most acute and hostile critics as companions, it is not surprising that K. and Amalia do not become close comrades or bosom friends. It would not be far-fetched to say that in the personalities of K. and Amalia Kafka has presented distorted images of social rebellion that are incomplete in complementary ways.

Patching together the desirable traits of each, and adding the circumstance that both K. and Amalia orient their life-projects around a response to indignities suffered at the hands of political authority, one would be constructing the image of a person who joins with others in principled fashion to protest commonly felt wrongs—an idealized political activist, in short. Such a citizen would resolve the false dichotomy of autonomy and isolation versus community and submission that has trapped in confusion K. and Amalia and indeed all the villagers. For abstractly one can visualize a striving for autonomy that is compatible with a genuine and openly expressed need for community, of the sort that would take shape among villagers cajoled or otherwise assisted into principled rejection of Castle mistreatment of its subjects, as for instance Sortini's deplorable conduct toward Amalia. Once again I do not mean to say that Kafka affirms this positive ideal of citizen independence, but his portrayal of the characters of Amalia and K. shows such a sensitive awareness of their inadequacies as willy-nilly to *imply* the affirmation of a character capable of surmounting these faults. K.'s personal impasse is not destiny.

These reflections on Amalia and K. presuppose that an opposi-tional attitude toward the Castle is appropriate, and there have not been lacking commentators who, sensible of the religious dimension of the novel, have denied this presupposition. One of the strongest critical arguments aimed at showing that Kafka's deep sympathies lie with the Castle authorities rather than with those who challenge Castle authority is the assertion that K. undergoes a change of heart at the end of the novel. This change of heart on K.'s part is supposed to involve his reconciliation with Castle ways and the repudiation of his past aggressive behavior toward the Castle. These changes in K. are said to be first observable when he happens to encounter Bürgel, a Castle official who in a dreamlike sequence seems to offer K. the hope that any request he should now make regarding his case would be granted. Falling asleep as Bürgel articulates this offer, K. is at least half-aware that he is neglecting a fairy-tale opportunity for success, so his neglect signals that he is no longer so fully identified with the project of aggressive striving against the Castle, particularly with the small-child fantasy aspect of that quest. K., it is said, is becoming religiously mature. K.'s demeanor after the Bürgel interview is greatly subdued. He is no longer inclined to voice legalistic objections to Castle proceedings or to balk at any prima facie unfairness in the treatment he receives at the hands of the Castle. Hostility toward Castle authority and personal ambition to rise in the Castle hierarchy seem equally to have vanished from K.'s mind. Summarizing these points, Ronald Gray writes, this novel is "about a man's entry into a state of grace."

In keeping with my general approach to the novel, I want to distinguish sharply between the issue of whether K. actually does undergo a transformation of the sort outlined above, and the issue of whether Kafka expects the reader unreservedly to sympathize with any such turnabout in K.

On the first issue, I believe it is moot whether K. suddenly recognizes a mysterious benevolence in the Castle authorities whom he had once believed to be implacably hostile. Most of K.'s subdued behavior at the end of the novel falls into place readily if we keep in mind that he is exhausted from exertion and lack of sleep. His passivity, his momentary aimlessness, and his submissiveness in the face of rebuke are all explicable in terms of his fatigue, so it is otiose to drag in the hypothesis of a fundamental alteration in K.'s attitudes to explain his behavior. The one event that is at least apparently recalcitrant to this fatigue explanation is the long conversation with Pepi near the story's close, for this conversation occurs after K. has refreshed himself with a long nap in the taproom. This conversation will bear careful examination, for the change-of-heart interpretation we are presently considering must rest upon its evidence.

This conversation leaves an impression that is incompatible with the assertion that K. is a man who is newly arrived into a state of grace. K.'s attitude is still more one of fatigue than of beatific calm. It has been said that in Pepi's chatter K. must recognize a reflection of the hostile, greedy, and paranoid mentality he himself exhibited in his first dealings with people after arriving in the village. Surely this judgment unfairly characterizes the K. of the opening chapters of the story. At the onset of the story K. is suspicious and somewhat flamboyantly intent on arranging a confrontation with the Castle over some matter of high principle, but the story soon reveals that K.'s suspicion is far from groundless and that the style of Castle administration would provoke any reasonable man to principled confrontation. If it is unfair to overemphasize the similarity of K. and Pepi, it must be noted that K. himself is guilty of this undiscriminating assimilation when he contrasts his and Pepi's aggressive ambition with Frieda's more admirable patience. Addressing Pepi, K. says:

> When I compare myself with you, something of this kind dawns on me: it is as if we had both striven too intently, too noisily, too childishly, with too little experience, to get something that with Frieda's calm and Frieda's matter-of-factness can be got easily and without much ado.

In likening himself to Pepi, K. ignores any element in his own character that posed a moral challenge to the Castle. Perhaps he has changed his mind; perhaps he no longer believes he ever had a principled basis for challenging Castle authority. But it is relevant to observe that K.'s awareness of himself as a moral agent has been episodic all through the novel. At times, notably in his conversation with the village elder, K. sonorously identifies himself as a man of principle, but at other times, especially when mollifying Frieda, K. describes himself as a man who simply wants to get ahead in the world. Hence K.'s comment does not constitute decisive evidence that he has undergone a sudden crisis conversion, but it does suggest that if K. has changed, the changes may not be improvements.

K.'s testimonial to Frieda in the conversation with Pepi throws further light on his supposed great transformation. The contrast that he paints between Pepi and Frieda, and the image of Frieda that emerges from this contrast, are both garish and misleading. Frieda is not the saint recalled by K. His praise of Frieda is so wildly inflated that not even the mildly attentive reader can accept it at face value. It is utterly implausible to suggest, as critics do, that Frieda represents a more adequate model of religious striving than K. or Pepi have yet attained. In her hostility to the Barnabas family—to cite the gravest example bearing adversely on Frieda's character—Frieda shows herself to be a parrot of the worst prejudices of the village. Even more damaging to her reputation should be the important fact that she is a tale-bearer whose malicious gossip first brought the Barnabas family into disrepute. Properly understood, the contrast drawn between Pepi and Frieda is not a moral contrast at all, despite K.'s avowal, but rather a comparison of passive and skillful ambition such as Frieda's with aggressive and clumsy ambition such as Pepi's. K.'s critique of Pepi reduces to the observation that her strategies for getting ahead in the world have so far been unavailing. The reader will sense that now that Frieda is back in her position of minor status, close to Klamm, she appears more attractive to K.—hence his tendency to idealize her now. If K. means to be doing anything more than paying nostalgic tribute to a former mistress, if he means to uphold Frieda as an exemplar of the right way to live in the village, then his judgment is sentimentally blurred.

K. does make one chiding remark to Pepi that might seem to suggest a reassessment of his own case. He says that Pepi's view of the world, far from corresponding to the facts, is the pinched and narrow perspective of a servant peeping at her masters through keyholes. This remark might be thought to apply to K.'s own (preconversion) perspective on events. What K. understands now, the argument might run, is that his perceptions too are biassed by his interests, so a more tolerant and open-minded attitude is appropriate. No claim about the relativity of one's perceptions to one's social position, however, could justify a wholesale repudiation of one's own perceptions, much less a submission to authority motivated by discounting one's authority-challenging beliefs. After all, if the chambermaid's perception of the gentlefolk is likely distorted, by the same token so is the gentlefolk's perception of the chambermaid.

A particularly striking example of the incommensurability of the perceptions of Castle gentlemen and village commoners is given in the interview K. has with Erlanger, just at the time of K.'s alleged conversion. From the point-of-view of a common-sense observer of village affairs, Erlanger's way of looking at the issue of Frieda's possible return to the Herrenhof is monstrously distorted. Erlanger says that Frieda's presence before Klamm is like a smudge of dirt on his table, perfectly insignificant in itself, but familiar, therefore to be kept in its place pending any sign of a desire on Klamm's part for its removal. Compared to a merely possible irritation suffered by Klamm, the feelings and interests of Frieda are to be weighed as no more significant than a smudge of dirt, for the purposes of deciding what is to be done in a matter affecting both parties. A plainer statement that villagers are not fully human in the eyes of the Castle could scarcely be imagined. For K. to come to share Erlanger's view of these proceedings would be for him to adopt a perspective within which his own human dignity counts for very little.

In short, it is an open question whether K.'s life outlook shifts dramatically at the close of the novel. What cannot be in doubt is that evidence of the inhumanity of official Castle policies continues to mount at the end of the story, so even if K. myopically misses the significance of this evidence, Kafka plainly intends the reader should form his own judgment of K.'s myopia.

So far I have spoken of a three-termed relation between K., the Castle, and the village, as though the presence of all three in the novel were unproblematic, but there is some evidence that the second term of this relation ultimately ought to drop out of the analysis, since the elusiveness of all description of the Castle indicates it is simply a reification of the villagers' psychological inadequacies. That is, the villagers posit a sublime Castle to justify their undignified subservience to civil authority. In so doing, the villagers are involved in a self-deception which will bedevil any commentator who accepts the Castle as anything more than the creation of myth or fantasy. Without laying to rest the charge that my own commentary has been too gullible in this respect, my political interpretation of the novel may seem to repose on assumptions open to doubt.

Is the Castle a real political authority or a ghostly image of the villagers' incapacity for self-governance? One way to appreciate the impact of this question on a proper understanding of the novel is to consider in what circumstances an attitude like the village elder's toward his political superiors would be justifiable—or at least excusable. The answer that suggests itself is that if one were the subject of an insecure but fearsome dictatorship, under whose rule official repression might be visited upon anybody at any time without any adherence to fair legal procedures, devoting one's life to staying in the good graces of the authorities at all costs might be a reasonable strategy for survival. The village elder behaves as it would be prudent to behave in order to escape notice during a reign of terror. This is not to say that in such adverse circumstances the mayor's cautious obeisance could not be faulted: even citizens of the most dictatorial regimes have the responsibility to resist their unjust authority, but it is a tricky matter to state exactly in what their responsibilities consist.

Is the world of *The Castle* cast in this harshly authoritarian mold? Kafka arranges a delicate balance of evidence pro and con. On the one side, the mayor's description of the Castle officialdom sounds very reminiscent of a satire directed against a ponderous and arbitrary statist bureaucracy. The plainest intrusions of the Castle into village life are the sexual forays of Castle officials, and in these episodes one discerns signs of an invidious caste hierarchy with distinct moralities for the rulers and the ruled biassed toward the interests of the rulers. These same forays illustrate an intrusion of public authority into what are normally the most private areas of life, which suggests that in the village there is no recognized sphere of private existence felt to be exempt from the meddling of Castle officials.

On the other side, Kafka introduces shadings and ambiguities which forestall any lurid or melodramatic interpretations of the political evidence. Any verdict on the dictatorial or totalitarian character of the Castle would have to be very severely hedged and qualified. There is evidently much passivity in the relation of the Castle toward the village. The Castle and its officials are more frequently described as acted upon than as acting. A single act of disobedience by K. seems to create consternation among the officials. No apparatus of state violence for quelling village unrest would appear to be at the disposal of the Castle. Indeed there are striking incidents showing Castle gentlemen to be peculiarly vulnerable to the unexpected behavior of the villagers. It is said that K.'s stubborn waiting for Klamm in the courtyard delayed that official's departure for two hours, since he was desirous of avoiding any meeting with K. Why on earth did not Klamm simply order K. forcibly removed from the courtyard? The Bürgel interview reveals a similar vulnerability in Castle officials. (However, perhaps the Bürgel incident gives a clue to the explanation of this apparent vulnerability, namely that it is only apparent and never leads to defeat for the Castle on any issue of consequence.)

Furthermore, the whole issue of the dictatorial character of Castle authority might seem to be undercut by the nagging doubt that the Castle literally does not exist at all. If the Castle does not exist apart from the villagers' imaginings, then responsibility for the degrading features of village life must rest squarely on the villagers themselves. If the Castle does exist and if it poses a dictatorial threat to the village, then a moralistic sneering at the cringing manner in which the villagers try to cope with this threat is out of place.

Although the above way of posing the issues is plausible, I believe it involves the error of exaggerating the significance of the question about the Castle's literal existence or nonexistence. After all, whether the structure that sits above the village is a fantasy or a genuine castle or a ramshackle building of no significance, the Castle hierarchy is undeniably a real presence in the ongoing life of the village. Even on the most extreme voluntarist interpretation, which would represent the Castle as merely the creation of the villagers, actively sustained by their corrupt psychological needs, it is not the case that any individual villager could resist the Castle with impunity, much less with any hope of success. So sympathy with village timidity (as well as the determination to overcome it) is in order even for a reader who takes the harshest view of village life. Whether or not the Castle exists, the rule of the Castle exists, and needs to be made over into a form of governance more fitting to human life.

Moreover, the very presence of religious themes in the novel provides a ground for insisting on the authoritarian character of Castle rule. The most natural explanation of the villagers' deification of political authority is that this ruling agency is arbitrary and capricious. It is psychologically easier to mystify an authority rather than to acknowledge the harsh fact that one's life is under the dominion of an arbitrary, perhaps evil power. Kafka's great achievement in this novel is to have shown how much suspicion and enmity are engendered in even the simplest human relations by the adoption of this mystifying attitude to civil authority. It is not just power that corrupts; powerlessness corrupts as well, by reproducing in people an abject dependence on authority that renders severely difficult the establishment of decent human community. K. is caught up in this syndrome even as he resists it.

Texts, Textuality, and Silence in Franz Kafka's *The Castle*

Marjanne E. Goozé

The understanding and interpretation of texts, papers, documents, and even of narration are central elements in Franz Kafka's novel *Das Schloβ* [*The Castle*]. Texts and textual interpretation present a problematic in the novel which impacts upon the critical analysis of the novel itself. Texts in *Das Schloβ,* including all written items and some narratives, represent the authority of the Castle with its bureaucratic, confusing, and hierarchical structure. In order to exist within this closed system, incorporating the village and the Castle, it appears necessary to understand these written items and narratives. This understanding, K. believes, should be achieved through correct interpretation and evaluation. K. searches for this correct interpretative method because he wishes to become a part of this system. Amalia, on the other hand, presents a possible alternative to the interpretative problem in her refusal to interpret, in the sense that interpretation is a means of gaining an absolute understanding of the Castle. She denies this method of interpretation because it does not question the structures of the system or of interpretation.

The events in the novel and Kafka's text demand an active, questioning interpretation. This must be approached on two levels: first, from within the text, the story of K. and his striving to interpret and understand the Castle; and second, from the perspective

From *MLN* 98, no. 3 (April 1983). © 1983 by The John Hopkins University Press. All translations of *Das Schloss, Der Prozess,* and "Das Schweigen der Sirenen" are by Willa and Edwin Muir. The translation of the passage from "Er" is by Christina Büchmann.

of the reader, who is confronted with similar problems when attempting to interpret Kafka's text, the novel itself. Texts and textuality will be examined from three aspects: content, what the text factually communicates; intent, what the author meant when writing; and form, the actual presentation of words on paper and the significance of the formality of writing. Textuality is used here to refer to the whole system of the production, distribution, and interpretation of texts in the novel.

K. receives two letters from Klamm, the first shortly after arriving in the village, the second somewhat later. Several other experiences with interpretation and texts intervene, altering K.'s view of letters as a means of exchanging information. By examining the way K. interprets, one can see the difficulties encountered in this process. Upon receiving the letter K. is struck by its apparent official nature. It serves to confirm his position in the service of the Castle. He believes he has been hired as surveyor: "K. hatte sich gemeldet, und seither wußte er, wie sich der Brief ausdrückte, daß er aufge-nommen war [K. had reported his arrival, and only after that, as the letter pointed out, had he known he was engaged]." He comes to this conclusion after reading the letter through several times in the privacy of his room. K. goes through the letter line by line, analyzing the importance and meaning of each individual word. He is looking for a specific content that can be deduced from a careful reading. He recognizes that there are difficult passages, but basically he has no difficulty in deciphering the letter. His major problem with the letter is the illegible signature. K. feels that he needs to know who the author of this text is. K.'s interpretation ultimately relies upon the authority of the author. If he is to evaluate the sig-nificance of the letter, to place it in a hierarchical structure, he must know the status of the author in that structure. Barnabas, who delivered the letter says that he has not read it, but he knows its origin—it comes from Klamm, whose name resounds through the novel with authority.

The letter is important to K. not only as communication between the Castle and himself, but also as text. K. has a tremendous respect for official papers. Written texts or oral, narrated texts, are far more important than visual perceptions. He takes down one of the pictures in the maid's room where he is staying and hangs the letter in its place on the wall: "in diesem Zimmer würde er wohnen, hier sollte der Brief hängen [This was the room he was to live in, and the letter should hang there]." The letter hangs in place of an icon. K. has canonized words on paper.

K.'s interpretation of Klamm's letter is challenged by the Mayor. With Mizzi's assistance the Mayor determines Klamm as the writer of the letter, but evaluates its significance differently than K., even though he uses the same interpretative method. The letter is not then an official document, but a private letter. K. learns from the Mayor that the letter still has meaning: " 'Ein Privatbrief Klamms hat natürlich viel mehr Bedeutung als eine amtliche Zuschrift; nur die Bedeutung, die *Sie* ihm beilegen, hat er nicht [A private letter from Klamm has naturally far more significance than an official letter, but it isn't precisely the kind of significance that you attach to it].' " Although their method of interpreting is primarily *werkimmanent*, they falter in applying categories such as "public" and "private" which do not function in this society. K. has already noticed this: "Nirgends noch hatte K. Amt und Leben so verflochten gesehen wie hier, so verflochten, daß es manchmal scheinen konnte, Amt und Leben hätten ihre Plätze gewechselt [Never yet had K. seen vocation and life so interlaced as here, so interlaced that sometimes one might think that they had exchanged places]." The Mayor makes these distinctions as well. Despite their knowledge of this society, they do not apply these categories to the letter, but they do this while seeking to use texts as a means to an end in this society. The problem of content may spring just as much from the "meaning" which ambitious readers attach to it as from textual ambiguity.

Since interpreting with little outside information can lead to contradictory interpretations, it is necessary to look at these texts, which are in themselves ambiguous, not only from the standpoint of the information they impart, but also from the standpoint of what they or their authors intend to tell us. This presents difficulties, as these authors remain unavailable to clarify their writings. It is possible that these texts are deliberately ambiguous. Judgment of intent in *Das Schloß* is accomplished with as little information as the evaluation of content. Without access to the author of these letters and documents one is still interpreting blindly. Olga explains to K. the intent of Sortini's note to Amalia in these terms: " 'Der Brief an Amalia kann ja im Gedanken, in völliger Nichtachtung des wirklich geschriebenen auf das Papier geworfen sein [The letter to Amalia may have been the thought of a moment, thrown on the paper in complete disregard for the meaning to be taken out of it].' " She just assumes this, just as K. assumes that the letter he receives is official.

If both the content and the intent of these texts are not unquestionably decipherable, then the importance that these documents possess lies solely in their existence as document, in their form. One also begins to realize that this is perhaps how these documents should be viewed, since they are only created as a formality. A protocol was taken of the meeting between the Mayor and K. The teacher, who also handles the written work required by the Castle for the Mayor, tells K. that it was only taken, " 'weil bei uns in allem strenge Ordnung sein muβ [because with us everything must be done in strict order].' " K. too is beginning to realize that the creation of documents is merely a formality, as he refuses to answer Momus's questions for his protocol for Klamm. In fact, Klamm does not read any protocols. This leaves K. in a double bind, in an apparently paradoxical situation where he cannot win. His only officially acknowledged means of communicating with Klamm is through documents; yet Klamm does not read these documents, and it is even doubtful that the letters K. receives come directly from Klamm. When K. receives the second letter from Klamm he becomes more aware of the inefficacy of letters as a means of communication here. At this point in the novel, however, his faith in the bureaucratic system of the Castle remains intact and his respect for papers unchallenged.

In hanging Klamm's first letter on the wall K. shows utmost respect for written documents. Even as he begins to realize that these have no informational value, he still respects them and expects others to do so as well. The protocol which appears so important to Momus is desecrated in K.'s eyes by Momus eating a pretzel with his beer, "mit der er alle Papiere mit Salz und Kümmel überstreute [in the process all the papers becoming covered with salt and caraway seeds]." In the episode with the Mayor K. gets an opportunity to see what happens to these papers no one reads. They get stuffed haphazardly into a cabinet or a hay loft. Only in their abundance lies their value. K. is just as shocked as Mizzi when she opens the cabinet: "Beim Öffnen rollten zwei große Aktenbündel heraus, welche rund gebunden waren, so wie man Brennholz zu binden pflegt. . . . Die Papier bedeckten schon das halbe Zimmer [When it was opened two large packages of papers rolled out, tied in round bundles, as one usually binds firewood. . . . The papers now covered half the floor]." Perhaps their true usefulness would be to use them as

ciency of the system. He cannot completely accept the meaningless-
ness of the documents because that would also require him to
question the existence of the governing system of the Castle. This he
is not prepared to do, and, as will be discussed later, this is exactly
what Amalia does when she tears up Sortini's note. K. is, however,
only slightly dismayed when the last note is torn up after the
distribution of the documents: "Es war wohl die erste Unregelmäß-
igkeit, die K. hier im Bürobetrieb gesehen hatte, allerdings war es
möglich, daß er sie unrichtig verstand [It was probably the first
irregularity that K. had seen in the working of the administration
here; admittedly it was possible that he had misunderstood this
too]." K. is still attempting to understand the Castle, to penetrate its
secrets. His dismay comes from the thought that the destroyed slip
of paper could have related to him.

The only character who has no relationship to paper is Pepi. K.
feels it would be preferable to be a maid and be close to papers than
to work in the bar. But it is exactly this proximity, and the suspicion
that the maids steal the papers, from which she wishes to escape. She
tells K.: " 'Was machen sich die Mädchen aus Akten? [What did the
maids care about files?].' " In the bar it is conversation, and not the
distribution and handling of documents, that takes place. For Pepi,
the spoken word is primary. She believes in the magic of speech. It
is perhaps for this reason that her talk with K. is related by Kafka
indirectly and not, like Olga's narrative, in quotation marks. Olga's
narrative is not only about texts and letters, but is itself a text;
whereas Pepi's flow of speech is related indirectly and is not itself a
text, but is part of the larger narrative. K. does not believe what Pepi
tells him, but he believes Olga. Pepi is also unimportant to K.
because she is not even interested in these matters. She therefore has
no connection with the Castle, which remains his ultimate goal.

Although K. turns away from Pepi because she is not connected
with textuality, he has failed to see that no women in the village
control papers. Olga's narrative is a text, a kind of verbal document,
but because it lacks the official stamp and signature of the Castle, K.
discounts it. Women's language lacks the tie to the power he
pursues. He is more interested in Olga's connections to the officials
she meets at the Herrenhof, attempting to use the women of the
village to gain personal access to the officials. His goal is to speak to
Klamm directly. It appears that K.'s philosophy is similar to Josef
K.'s in *Der Prozeß* [*The Trial*]. The prison chaplain tells Josef K.:

firewood. This same abundance presents itself in the
description of Sortini's office, with its pillars of documents \
constantly toppling over.

The possession of mountains of papers seems to gi
minor officials importance. K. perceives that those who p(
are allowed to examine documents are initiated into the mys
this system. At the Mayor's K. is not permitted to assist in
through the papers, although his assistants are: "Was K. nich
die Gehilfen durften es [What had not been permitted to
allowed to the assistants]." This places them higher in the
than K., who really stands outside of it and is trying to get in
the highest possible level. While it is apparent that having ac
papers places one above individuals not permitted to deal wit
documents, those who are apparently in the highest positi
power do not handle papers. Authority for K. is coupled
beginning with possession of paper—a paper that would nan
surveyor—and the person who can provide him with that
Klamm. It appears, however, that Klamm, who does not re
protocols, does not work like Sortini. His desk in the Herren
empty. When K. looks through the peephole he is looking j
much for papers as at Klamm:

> [D]a die Randseite des Tisches hoch war, konnte K. nicht
> genau sehen, ob dort irgendwelche Schriften lagen, es
> schien ihm aber, als wäre er leer. Der Sicherheit halber bat
> er Frieda, durch das Loch zu schauen und ihm darüber
> Auskunft zu geben. Da sie vor kurzem im Zimmer
> gewesen war, konnte sie K. ohne weiteres bestätigen, daß
> dort keine Schriften lagen. [There was a rim round the
> desk which prevented K. from seeing whether any papers
> were lying on it; he had the idea, however, that there were
> none. To make it certain, he asked Frieda to look through
> the hole and tell him if there were any. But as she had been
> in that very room a short time ago, she was able to inform
> him without further ado that the desk was empty.]

Bürgel, who is important to K. at the end of the novel, does n
receive any papers when they are distributed in the Herrenhof.

Even at this late stage in *Das Schloβ*, K. is still fascinated by tl
distribution of documents, although he is well aware of the ineff

" 'Du suchst zuviel fremde Hilfe . . . und besonders bei Frauen [You cast about too much for outside help . . . especially from women],' " but Josef K. insists: " 'Die Frauen haben eine große Macht. Wenn ich einige Frauen, die ich kenne, dazu bewegen könnte, gemeinschaftlich für mich zu arbeiten, müßte ich durchdringen [Women have great influence. If I could move some women I know to join forces in working for me, I couldn't help winning through].' "

K. seeks out those in the village who he believes have connections with the Castle. Except for Amalia his relationship with the female characters is sexual; and with Barnabas, official. As K. has no personal access to Klamm, all the information he receives about him comes from these sources. Of utmost importance is the messenger Barnabas, who brings K. letters from Klamm. Barnabas appears to K. more important than the assistants. His white clothing also makes him stand out, as if he were dressed in paper. Amalia disapproves of her brother's service to the Castle. Having earlier insulted a Castle messenger, she denies both the authority of the Castle and that of the messenger bearing the letter, since he represents its sender. The sender here appears to be the Castle. This transference of authority and affections is exemplified in the picture of the messenger that Gardena keeps with her. This messenger was " 'der Bote, durch den Klamm mich zum ersten Male zu sich berief [the messenger that Klamm sent to call me to him the first time].' " Messengers serve in the novel both to further distance relationships and to form the communicational ties between the Castle and the village or between the Castle and K. Considering the actual lack of communication, the fact that no significant information is usually exchanged, this tie is purely symbolic.

It is the act of delivering or receiving a letter that matters and not the content. K. realizes this by the time he receives the second letter, but by no means does he devalue the importance of this event. He tells Frieda about Barnabas: " 'Er kommt selten, und was er bringt ist belanglos, nur daß es geradewegs von Klamm herrührt, macht es wertvoll [He comes very seldom, and what messages he brings are of no importance; only the fact that they come from Klamm gives them any value].' " He does not question the basic authority of the Castle, he has only learned that the paper system does not function flawlessly. Upon receiving the second letter outside in the wind and snow, he tells Barnabas regarding the letter: " 'Es ist ein Mißverständnis [There's been a misunderstanding].' " Yet, he still has faith that these mistakes and misunderstandings can be straightened out. He gives Barnabas a message for Klamm to be delivered orally: " 'aber du mußt es doch mündlich ausrichten, einen Brief will ich nicht schreiben, er würde ja doch eben den endlosen Aktenweg gehen [but you must learn it by heart, I don't want to write a letter, it would only go the same endless way as the other papers].' " K. attempts, like Klamm, to avoid documents.

By ordering Barnabas to speak directly to Klamm, K. is attempting to cut through a distancing layer between himself and the authorities, to place himself one step closer to direct contact with Klamm. Speaking with Klamm, the highest known authority in the Castle who is in some way present in the novel is K.'s goal: " 'aber das wichtigste ist doch für mich, daß ich ihm gegenüberstehe [but still the most important thing for me is to be confronted with him].' " He believes speaking with Klamm would solve his problems regarding his job as surveyor, his relationship with Frieda, and meeting Klamm would also raise him to a position of power and authority in this society. K. desires not merely to be accepted into this society, but to immediately attain high status within it. He does not wish to relinquish his independence in order to accomplish this. Entry into this society at a high level he feels might allow him to retain his independence. It is, however, quite apparent to the reader that K. is not going to have this opportunity, precisely because of his acceptance of the system. He is both unwilling and unable to really peel away these distancing layers, because his final goal is to manipulate and have power within the established structures.

After giving his oral message to Barnabas, K. reflects: "K. hatte in Selbstvergessenheit gesprochen, so, als stehe er vor Klamms Tür und spreche mit dem Türhüter [K. had forgotten himself while he was speaking, it was as if he were standing before Klamm's door talking to the porter]." This is a direct parallel to the parable "Vor dem Gesetz" ["Before the Law"] told by the prison chaplain in *Der Prozeß*. This parallel lies not only between K. and the "Mann vom Lande [Man from the Country]," as K. does eventually enter at least into Bürgel's room, but especially in the interpretation of these actions by the chaplain. For, the chaplain in *Der Prozeß* interprets the parable using the same method that both K. and the Mayor use, and arrives at two different and contradictory conclusions.

Attempting to disentangle these conflicting interpretations of the text, and of every event in *Das Schloß*, only leads one deeper into its traps. The reader, like K., is given no omniscient perspective from which to judge the events in the novel. Due to this lack of narrative perspective the reader does not know what is "true." Like K., the reader is subjected to these long conversations, where one contradicts the other, or, because of the extensive use of subjunctive mood, everything remains pure speculation. Most of what K. and the reader learn about the Castle is derived from hearsay. An example of this is when Olga tells K. what she heard from Barnabas about the Castle offices. The interpreter of Kafka's text is also left with almost no verifiable content, and little intent (Kafka's criticism of bureaucratic society is, however, unquestionably in the text). The reader has only the form "text," "novel," etc. and very little else to analyze that is not speculative. The layers of the text tend to hinder interpretation. The question must then be raised, how is one to deal with such a text? There are alternatives to K.'s method of interpretation. One of them is pointed to in *Das Schloß* by Amalia, who questions form, and therefore the whole system of textuality.

Amalia's story, which is told to K. by Olga, centers around her refusal to participate in this paper system. Her story has a substantial physical place in the novel, forming about one-sixth of the total book. It is more than just another episode. It offers an alternative view of this society which K. so desperately wants to become a part of. Amalia has rejected text to such a degree that she does not tell her own story to K., for this kind of narration creates a text. Olga gives K. three reasons for telling him Amalia's story. One of them is that Amalia instructed her to do so. The reader is not a party to these instructions and must remain aware that it is only Olga's interpretation which is presented. One should also be wary of making assumptions regarding Amalia's feelings and motives which are not firmly grounded in the text. Amalia's silence, the narration of Olga, and K.'s evaluation of this story are all connected to Amalia's initial act of denial.

Amalia is admired by Sortini at the festival. The following day he sends her a letter. She receives this letter very differently than K. receives his letter from Klamm. Amalia does not wish to be alone with it, read it many times, or canonize it. Olga also reads the letter. She is like the assistants, who read Klamm's second letter over K.'s shoulder and come to a different evaluation of the letter than K. She relates to K. Amalia's reception of the letter:

Am nächsten Morgen wurden wir aus unserem Weinschlaf durch einen Schrei Amalias geweckt. . . . Sie stand beim Fenster und hielt einen Brief in der Hand, den ihr eben ein Mann durch das Fenster gereicht hatte, der Mann wartete auf Antwort. Amalia hatte den Brief—er war kurz—schon gelesen und hielt ihn in der schlaff hinabhängenden Hand. . . . Ich kniete neben ihr nieder und las so den Brief. Kaum war ich fertig, nahm ihn Amalia, nach einem kurzen Blick auf mich wieder auf, brachte es aber nicht mehr über sich, ihn zu lesen, zerriß ihn, und warf die Fetzen dem Mann draußen ins Gesicht und schloß das Fenster. Das war jener entscheidende Morgen. [Next morning we were roused from our heavy sleep by a scream from Amalia. . . . She was standing by the window holding a letter in her hand which had just been passed in through the window by a man who was still waiting for an answer. The letter was short, and Amalia had already read it, and held it in her drooping hand. . . . I knelt down beside her and read the letter. Hardly had I finished it when Amalia after a brief glance at me took it back, but she couldn't bring herself to read it again, and, tearing it in pieces, she threw the fragments in the face of the man outside and shut the window. That was the morning which decided our fate.]

In her act of defiance she refuses to interpret at all. By tearing up the letter she denies the patriarchal authority of the Castle. She refuses to play the game. The point is also clearly made by Olga, that Amalia had other alternatives which would have enabled her to avoid going to Sortini without challenging the system itself: " 'Es gab manche Auswege. . . . Hätte sie nur irgendwie zum Schein gefolgt [There were many ways of getting around it. . . . If she had only made some pretence of compliance].' " Amalia breaks with all form by destroying the paper, insulting the messenger, and refusing to go to Sortini.

She is an exception to all the assumptions made within this society. By denying its structure, she is beyond the understanding of those within this closed system. This becomes evident when one looks at Olga's assumption, " 'daß Frauen nicht anders können als Beamte lieben, wenn sich diese ihnen einmal zuwenden [that women can't help loving the officials once they give them any encouragement].' " Olga understands Amalia's outrage at Sortini's crudely written letter, but she cannot accept that Amalia does not love Sortini. She tells K.:

> Aber Amalia ist eine Ausnahme, wirst du sagen. Ja, das ist sie, das hat sie bewiesen, als sie sich weigerte, zu Sortini zu gehen, das ist der Ausnahme genug; daß sie nun aber außerdem Sortini auch nicht geliebt haben sollte, das wäre nun schon der Ausnahme zuviel, das wäre gar nicht mehr zu fassen. [But Amalia's an exception, you will say. Yes, that she is, that she has proved in refusing to go to Sortini, that's exception enough; but if in addition she weren't in love with Sortini, she would be too exceptional for plain human understanding.]

Within the system Amalia's act is incomprehensible. Olga recognizes that within the system Amalia has to be despised and at the same time realizes the significance of her act: " 'Sie ist gar nicht zu verteidigen, sondern nur zu loben [She's not to be defended, but only to be praised].' " She is deserving of praise because she rejects the paper system.

Most critics fail to recognize this. She does not, as Walter Sokel asserts, confirm the rule that all women love officials, because the force of her rejection indicates how much she is influenced by Sortini. There is no basis upon which to ground this statement, except upon Olga's speculation (cited above) which is formulated in the subjunctive. Nor are there any indications in the text that Amalia is overly proud or denying her "female nature" in her rejection of the official. All the other women in the novel are willing to enter into sexual relationships with officials, except Amalia and Gisa, the teacher. But Gisa, in having Schwarzer at her feet, just reverses the roles. She does not open up the system. If this may be women's nature, it is not discussed in the text. It is true only of most of the female characters in the novel. Women's sexual oppression is required by the system, and it should by no means be raised to the level of religious allegory as is done by Max Brod and Erich Heller. This kind of interpretation does not take cognizance of the alternative to the textual and sexual order of the Castle that Amalia offers.

Most critics fail to recognize this. She does not, as Walter Sokel
The alternative which Amalia presents has grave consequences.

Amalia sees through the structure of the system and understands the significance of her act. Even Olga is aware of this. She states:

> Aber Amalia trug nicht nur das Leid, sondern hatte auch den Verstand, es zu durchschauen, wir sahen nur die Folgen, sie sah in den Grund, wir hofften auf irgendwelche kleinen Mittel, sie wußte, daß alles entschieden war, wir hatten zu flüstern, she hatte nur zu schweigen, Aug in Aug mit der Wahrheit stand sie und lebte und ertrug dieses Leben damals wie heute. [But Amalia not only suffered, but had the understanding to see her suffering clearly; we saw only the effects, but she knew the cause, we hoped for some small relief or other, she knew that everything was decided, we had to whisper, she had only to be silent. She stood face to face with the truth and went on living and endured her life then as now.]

Amalia's choice takes tremendous courage, since she has no hope of either being joined by other members of this society in her denial or of escaping completely from the closed system of the village. She is isolated. Her family stands by her for a while, ceding to her the leadership of the family. But even they must betray her because they cannot live without hope. Olga recognized their betrayal: " 'Wir verrieten Amalia, wir rissen uns los von ihrem schweigenden Befehl, wir konnten nicht mehr so weiterleben, ganz ohne Hoffnung konnten wir nicht leben [We betrayed Amalia, we shook off her silent restraint, we couldn't go on living like that, without hope of any kind we could not live].' " This hope is tied to the structure of the Castle. If one rejects its domination, one must be prepared to pay the price.

Amalia is the only character in *Das Schloß* who stands outside of the Castle's domination. Her denial is a first step in opening up this closed society; it is especially powerful because she still lives in the village and has not been destroyed by her act. A passage from Kafka's work "Er" ["He"] points to this:

> Die Kraft zum Verneinen, dieser natürlichsten Äußerung des immerfort sich verändernden, erneuernden, absterben-den, auflebenden menschlichen Kämpferorganismus, ha-ben wir immer, den Mut aber nicht, während doch Leben Verneinen ist, also Verneinung Bejahung. [We still have

the strength to deny these most natural expressions of the human warrior organism that changes, renews itself, dies off, and revives, but we haven't the courage to do so, since to live is to deny, and that is negative affirmation.]

Amalia's significance is apparent to the reader but not to K. He attempts to find in Amalia a reflection of his own situation and is disappointed when he does not find it. He identifies more strongly with Olga's attempts to gain the forgiveness of the Castle. The choice between them would be clear. He does not see an alternative in Amalia because he does not wish to live outside the authority of the Castle. K. states: " 'Meine Angelegenheiten mit den Behörden in Ordnung zu bringen ist mein höchster, eigentlich mein einziger Wunsch [It's my most urgent wish, really my only wish, to get my business with the authorities properly settled].' " He will not relinquish his belief in the Castle and its ability to put his life in order. He still believes in the "Happy-End" that Amalia abjures. K., as surveyor, is not so much interested in drawing new boundaries as he is in discovering what the existing ones are. His surveying position is not a "revoluntionärer Akt [revolutionary action]" as Wilhelm Emrich postulates, nor is he even much interested in changing or overturning boundaries, as Heinz Politzer asserts [in *Franz Kafka: Der Künstler*]. His goal is to attain as high a position as possible within this system.

In the beginning K. sees in Amalia another clue to unlocking the secret of the Castle. Her gaze disturbs him from the moment he enters Barnabas's hut at the beginning of the novel: "Darin beirrte ihn nur Amalia ein wenig mit ihrem ernsten, geraden, unrührbaren, vielleicht auch etwas stumpfen Blick [Yet he was somewhat disturbed by Amalia's direct and serious gaze, which was unflinching and perhaps a little stupid]." Later in the novel he also notices her gaze: "Ihr Blick war kalt, klar, unbeweglich wie immer [Her gaze was cold, clear, and steady as usual]." From these observations one gets the impression of a cold and perhaps arrogant Amalia. It is her smile though that leads K. to believe she holds the secret to the Castle, which she does, but it is not the one he wishes to know:

Amalia lächelte, und dieses Lächeln, obwohl es traurig war, erhellte das düster zusammengezogene Gesicht, machte die Stummheit sprechend, machte die Fremdheit vertraut, war die Preisgabe eines Geheimnisses, die Preisgabe eines bisher gehüteten Besitzes, der zwar wieder zurückgenommen werden konnte, aber niemals mehr ganz. [Amalia smiled, and this smile of hers, though sad, lit up her gloomy face, made her silence eloquent, her strangeness intimate, and unlocked a mystery jealously guarded hitherto, a mystery that could indeed be concealed again, but never so completely.]

Her gaze and her smile are so important because of her silence. Except for her scream, uttered when she first read Sortini's letter, she has not spoken about her experience. Her silence is not a complete withdrawal from all communication; through her silence she indicates several things. It is a form of speaking which goes beyond language in that it points to the inability of this language to articulate her experience and her denial without her being absorbed back into the system. Silence is very much a legitimate response to an entrapping situation, since she is not permitted to physically leave this society.

That possibility appears to remain open to K. Frieda suggests leaving, but he replies: " 'Auswandern kann ich nicht . . . ich bin hierhergekommen, um hier zu bleiben. Ich werde hierbleiben [I can't go away. . . . I came here to stay. I'll stay].' " K. excludes the possibility of leaving in his own mind, thus entrapping himself in this society, because he still desires to be accepted into and to gain high status within it.

Amalia's silence disturbs K. because she refuses to mirror his own desires. Her silence is not a secret she is saving for herself, but the result of the society and its language. Her silence is not total, but she uses the language so ambiguously that K.'s attempts at absolute understanding fail. Her speech is as mysterious to him as her silence. She tells K. a kind of story about a man who pursued the Castle. He believes he would be interested in the man. Amalia realizes that K. would be interested in the woman and points this out to him. She understands him, but he is confused by her. Amalia is the only woman in *Das Schloß* to whom K. does not turn for help. Because she is not sexually tied to any official, she can be, in his mind, of no "use" to him. K.'s focus on Sortini and not on Amalia also prevents him from seeing her as an alternative, and perhaps even as a "Lösungsmöglichkeit [possible solution]," as Heinz Politzer terms the alternative Amalia offers. Amalia does not allow herself to be defined by the language of the Castle, as K. does in desiring to be officially sanctioned as surveyor. Olga says of her use of language: " 'Es ist nicht leicht, sie genau zu verstehen, weil man oft nicht weiß, ob sie ironisch oder ernst spricht. Meistens ist es ja ernst, aber es klingt ironisch [It is not easy to follow her, for often one can't tell whether she's speaking ironically or in earnest. Mostly she's in earnest but it sounds ironical].' "

Silence, however, is far more powerful than speech. K. does not want to hear Amalia's silence. He could not accept the consequences. In this way he is like Odysseus in Kafka's "Das Schweigen der Sirenen" ["The Silence of the Sirens"]:

> Nun haben aber die Sirenen eine noch shrecklichere Waffe als den Gesang, nämlich ihr Schweigen. Es ist zwar nicht geschehen, aber vielleicht denkbar, daß sich jemand vor ihrem Gesang gerettet hätte, vor ihrem Schweigen gewiß nicht. . . . Odysseus aber, um es so auszudrükken, hörte ihr Schweigen nicht, er glaubte, sie sängen, und nur er sei behütet es zu hören. [Now the Sirens have a still more fatal weapon than their song, namely their silence. And though admittedly such a thing has never happened, still it is conceivable that someone might possibly have escaped from their singing, but from their silence certainly never. . . . But Ulysses, if one may so express it, did not hear their silence; he thought they were singing and that he alone did not hear them.]

Amalia's silence is dangerous, but not so dangerous as Wilhelm Emrich and Klaus-Peter Philippi [in *Reflexion und Wirklichkeit*] believe, as to endanger the authoritarian existence of the Castle. Because she is isolated she poses no threat to its dominance, just as K. is not dangerous to the system because he wants to be absorbed by it. They have only given it a mild shock—Amalia by refusing to play within the system, and K. by doing the unexpected in seeing Bürgel. Further, there is a significant difference between Amalia's refusal and K.'s visit with Bürgel. K. is attempting to find a way into the bureaucratic machine, Amalia, a way out.

Amalia's denial of texts and textual systems points the way out of the binds of the novel for both K. and the reader. The problem lies in both recognizing the denial in her silence and accepting its consequences. Because Amalia is alone in her situation she must remain silent. Through her silence she points to the necessity of creating a new language or reforming the old in such a way that would permit her experience to be articulated. Her silence is a refusal to interpret as K. and the others do. This poses problems for the interpreter of Kafka's *Das Schloβ*. If one views Amalia's experience as an alternative to K.'s strivings, then one most forsake interpretation to a large degree. Viewing Amalia as an alternative also places the climax of the novel in the fifteenth chapter, which forces one to re-evaluate the importance of the episode with Bürgel. This episode then does not show to K. lost opportunities, but points out, on the other hand, how firmly entrenched K. is in the values of this system. It is clear that K. does not see in Amalia an alternative stance to this system because this alternative rejects this system and he does not.

Amalia's refusal to interpret affects, however, how an interpreter of Kafka's *Das Schloβ* handles the text. Kafka's text itself does not allow the reader to interpret as K. does, passively and never questioning the way one reads. The text, through the employment of subjunctive mood and extensive narrative layers, does not permit one to grasp the text as K. does Klamm's letters. If one attempts to interpret as K., one gets just as lost and confused as he. Kafka's text demands that the reader, like Amalia, actively question interpretation and even the form of the text itself. Kafka's *Das Schloβ* indicates to the careful reader the traps of traditional interpretation and the need to interpret differently, but does not really give the interpreter many clues as to how this new kind of interpretation is to be done or what it will look like. One is left solely with Amalia's refusal to interpret and her silence. Kafka's text shows the necessity of breaking out of traditional textual systems, points the way out, but offers no alternative solution to the problems of interpretation.

Chronology

1883	Franz Kafka born in Prague, July 3, to Hermann and Julie Löwy Kafka. Hermann, son of a Czech-Jewish country butcher's family, has risen, with the help of his wife's family, to establish his own business selling fancy goods. Franz's two brothers, born 1885 and 1887, both die in infancy. Three sisters, born 1889, 1890, 1892, later die in Nazi concentration camps.
1889–1901	Franz attends German elementary school and German Staatsgymnasium.
1901–6	Studies law at the German Karl-Ferdinand University in Prague.
1902	Meets Max Brod.
1905	Spends several weeks at a sanatorium, the first of many such stays, owing to chronic ill-health.
1906	Starts working in a law office as a secretary. Receives law degree. Embarks on his year of practical training in Prague law courts.
1907	Takes position with an insurance company, but complains that the long hours interfere with his writing.
1908	Eight prose pieces published under the title *Betrachtung* (*Meditation*). Accepts position with Workers' Accident Insurance Institute.
1909	Two sketches (originally part of "Description of a Struggle") published. Trip to Riva and Brescia (with Max and Otto Brod). "Die Aeroplane in Brescia" published.

1910	Five prose pieces published under the title *Betrachtung* (*Meditation*). Starts diary. Trip to Paris (with Max and Otto Brod). Visit to Berlin.
1911	Official trip to Bohemia. Trip (with Max Brod) to Switzerland, Italy, and France, writing travelogues. Becomes interested in Yiddish theater and literature. His family starts an asbestos factory, in which he is reluctantly involved at various times.
1912	Visits Leipzig and Weimar (with Max Brod). Meets Felice Bauer. *Meditation* published.
1913	"The Stoker" published (first chapter of work-in-progress *Amerika*). Visits Felice Bauer in Berlin. "The Judgment" published. Travels to Vienna and Italy.
1914	Engagement to Felice Bauer. Breaks off engagement. Visits Germany. Starts *The Trial*. Writes "In the Penal Colony."
1915	Reconciliation with Felice Bauer. *The Metamorphosis* published.
1916	Resumes writing after two years' silence: the fragments of "The Hunter Gracchus," "A Country Doctor," and other stories later included in *A Country Doctor*.
1917	Reengagement to Felice Bauer. Tuberculosis diagnosed. Takes extended sick leave. Engagement to Felice Bauer broken off again.
1918	Continued ill health. Intermittent stays at sanatoria.
1919	Brief engagement to Julie Wohryzek. "In the Penal Colony" and *A Country Doctor* (collection of stories) published. Writes "Letter to His Father."
1920	Begins correspondence with Milena Jesenská. Intermittent stays at sanatoria.
1921	After eight months of sick leave, goes back to work with the Workers' Accident Insurance Institute but has to take another leave two months later. "The Bucket Rider" published.
1922	Writes *The Castle,* "A Hunger Artist," "Investigations of a Dog." Breaks off relations with Milena Jesenská. Retires from Workers Accident Insurance Institute. "A Hunger Artist" published.

1923   Meets Dora Dymant and goes to live with her in Berlin.

1924   Moves back to Prague and then to Sanatorium Wiener Wald near Vienna. Dies at Sanatorium Kierling also near Vienna. Buried in Prague. Collection *A Hunger Artist* published shortly after his death.

Contributors

HAROLD BLOOM, Sterling Professor of the Humanities at Yale University, is the author of *The Anxiety of Influence, Poetry and Repression,* and many other volumes of literary criticism. His forthcoming study, *Freud: Transference and Authority,* attempts a full-scale reading of all of Freud's major writings. A MacArthur Prize Fellow, he is general editor of five series of literary criticism published by Chelsea House. During 1987–88, he served as Charles Eliot Norton Professor of Poetry at Harvard University.

KENNETH BURKE is the author of such crucial works of theoretical and practical criticism as *Permanence and Change, The Philosophy of Literary Form, A Grammar of Motives,* and *A Rhetoric of Motives.*

W. G. SEBALD teaches at the University of East Anglia.

RONALD GRAY is J. R. R. Tolkien Professor of English at Oxford. Among his many critical studies in German literature are *Goethe the Alchemist, The German Tradition in Literature, Brecht the Dramatist,* and *Kafka's Castle.*

ERICH HELLER, author of *The Ironic German, The Poet's Self and the Poem,* and *Die Wiederkehr der Unschuld,* was Professor of Humanities at Northwestern University, Evanston.

RICHARD J. ARNESON is Professor of Philosophy at the University of California at San Diego.

MARJANNE E. GOOZÉ is Assistant Professor of German at the University of Georgia.

Bibliography

Adams, Robert M. *Strains of Discord: Studies in Literary Openness*. Ithaca: Cornell University Press, 1958.

Alter, Maria Pospischil. "The Over-Certified Castle: Or Look Who Is Talking." *Perspectives in Contemporary Literature* 3 (1977): 5–11.

Amann, Jürg. *Franz Kafka*. Munich: Piper, 1983.

Anders, Günther. *Franz Kafka*. New York: Hillary House, 1960.

Arendt, Hannah. "Franz Kafka: A Revaluation." *Partisan Review* 11 (1944): 412–22.

Barthes, Roland. *Critical Essays*. Evanston, Ill.: Northwestern University Press, 1972.

Bataille, Georges. *Literature and Evil*. London: Caldor & Boyars, 1973.

Beck, Evelyn Tornton. *Kafka and the Yiddish Theatre*. Madison: University of Wisconsin Press, 1971.

Benjamin, Walter. *Illuminations*. New York: Harcourt, Brace & World, 1960.

Bernheimer, Charles. *Flaubert and Kafka: Studies in Psychopoetic Structure*. New Haven: Yale University Press, 1982.

———. "Watts in the Castle: The Aporetic Quest in Kafka and Beckett." *Newsletter of the Kafka Society of America* 6 (1982): 19–24.

Blanchot, Maurice. *The Space of Literature*. Lincoln: University of Nebraska Press, 1982.

Borges, Jorge Luis. "Kafka and His Precursors." In *Labyrinths*. New York: New Directions, 1964.

Braybrooke, Neville. "Celestial Castles: An Approach to Saint Teresa and Franz Kafka." *Dublin Review* 229 (1955): 427–45.

Bridgwater, Patrick. *Kafka and Nietzsche*. Bonn: Bouvier, 1974.

Brod, Max. Afterword to *Das Schloß* by Franz Kafka. Frankfurt a. M.: Fischer Taschenbuch Verlag, 1976.

———. *Franz Kafka*. New York: Schocken, 1960.

Brown, Russell E. "Kafka's *Schloss*: Movement between Village and Castle." In *Perspectives and Personalities: Studies in Modern German Literature Honoring Claude Hill,* edited by Ralph Ley, Maria Wagner, Joanna M. Ratych, and Kenneth Hughes. Heidelberg: Winter, 1978.

Camus, Albert. *The Myth of Sisyphus*. New York: Knopf, 1955.

Canetti, Elias. *Kafka's Other Trial*. New York: Schocken, 1982.

Caputo-Mayr, Marie Luise, ed. *Kafka-Symposium*. Berlin: Agora, 1978.

Church, Margaret. "Time and Reality in Kafka's *The Trial* and *The Castle*." *Twentieth Century Literature* 2 (1956): 62–69.

Cohn, Dorrit. "K. Enters the Castle: On the Change of Person in Kafka's Manuscript." *Euphorion* 62 (1968): 28–45.

———. *Transparent Minds: Narrative Modes for Presenting Consciousness in Fiction.* Princeton, N.J.: Princeton University Press, 1978.

Cohn, Ruby. " 'Watt' in the Light of *Das Schloβ.*" *Comparative Literature* 13 (1961): 154–66.

Corngold, Stanley. *The Fate of the Self.* New York: Columbia University Press, 1986.

Emrich, Wilhelm. *Franz Kafka: A Critical Study of His Writings.* New York: Ungar, 1968.

Flores, Angel, ed. *The Kafka Debate.* New York: Gordian Press, 1977.

———, ed. *The Kafka Problem.* New York: Octagon, 1963.

Flores, Angel, and Homer Swander, eds. *Franz Kafka Today.* Madison: University of Wisconsin Press, 1958.

Foulkes, A. P. *The Reluctant Pessimist: A Study of Franz Kafka.* Paris and The Hague: Mouton, 1967.

Goodman, Paul. *Kafka's Prayer.* New York: Vanguard, 1947.

Gray, Ronald. *Kafka's Castle.* Cambridge: Cambridge University Press, 1956.

———, ed. *Kafka: A Collection of Critical Essays.* Englewood Cliffs, N.J.: Prentice-Hall, 1962.

Greenberg, Martin. *The Terror of Art: Kafka and Modern Literature.* New York: Basic Books, 1968.

Grimes, Margaret. "Kafka's Use of Cue-Names: Its Importance for an Interpretation of *The Castle*." *The Centennial Review* 18 (1974): 221–30.

Hall, Calvin I., and Richard E. Lind. *Dreams, Life and Literature: A Study of Franz Kafka.* Chapel Hill: University of North Carolina Press, 1970.

Hamalian, Leo, ed. *Franz Kafka: A Collection of Criticism.* New York: McGraw-Hill, 1974.

Heller, Erich. *Kafka.* London: Fontana/Collins, 1974.

———. *The Disinherited Mind.* New York: Harcourt Brace Jovanovich, 1975.

Heller, Peter. *Dialectics and Nihilism.* Amherst: University of Massachusetts Press, 1966.

Hoffman, Anne Golumb. "Plotting the Landscape: Stories and Storytellers in *The Castle*." *Twentieth Century Literature* 27 (1981): 289–307.

Hughes, Kenneth, ed. *Franz Kafka: An Anthology of Marxist Criticism.* Hanover and London: New England University Press, 1981.

Janouch, Gustav. *Conversations with Kafka.* New York: Praeger, 1953.

Kafka-Studien. Series 5 in *New Yorker Studien zur Neueren Deutschen Literaturgeschichte.* New York: Lang, 1985.

Kafka-Symposion. Contributions by Jürgen Born, Ludwig Dietz, Malcolm Pasley, Paul Raabe, and Klaus Wagenbach. Berlin: Verlag Klaus Wagenbach, 1965.

Kartiganer, Donald M. " 'A Ceremony of the Usual Thing': Notes on Kafka's Development." *Criticism* 20 (1978): 43–65.

Klein, Alan. "Kafka's *The Castle*." *The Explicator* 42, no. 3 (1984): 43–45.

Kuna, Franz. *Franz Kafka: Literature As Corrective Punishment*. London: Elek Books, 1974.

———, ed. *On Kafka: Semi-Centenary Perspectives*. London: Elek Books, 1974.

Lukács, Georg. *Realism In Our Time: Literature and the Class Struggle*. New York: Harper & Row, 1971.

Modern Australian Literature 11, nos. 3/4 (Autumn 1978). Special issue on Kafka.

Mosaic 3, no. 4 (Summer 1970). Special issue on Kafka.

Nagel, Bert. *Franz Kafka*. Berlin: Schmidt, 1974.

Neider, Charles. *Kafka: His Mind and Art*. London: Routledge, 1949.

Neumeyer, Peter F., ed. *Twentieth Century Interpretations of* The Castle: *A Collection of Critical Essays*. Englewood Cliffs, N.J.: Prentice-Hall, 1969.

Nutting, Peter West. "Kafka's 'Strahlende Heiterkeit': Discursive Humor and Comic Narration in *Das Schloss*." *DVLG* 57 (1983): 651–78.

Ong, Walter J. "Kafka's Castle and the West." *Thought* 22 (1947): 439–60.

Osborne, Charles. *Kafka*. New York: Barnes & Noble, 1967.

Parry, Idris. Review of *Das Schloß*. *London Magazine* 1 (May 1954): 78–81.

Pascal, Roy. *The German Novel*. Manchester, Eng.: Manchester University Press, 1956.

———. *Kafka's Narrators: A Study of His Stories and Sketches*. Cambridge: Cambridge University Press, 1982.

Pawel, Ernst. *The Nightmare of Reason: A Life of Franz Kafka*. New York: Farrar, Straus, & Giroux, 1984.

Perry, Ruth. "Madness in Euripides, Shakespeare and Kafka: An Examination of the *Bacchae, Hamlet, King Lear,* and *The Castle*." *Psychoanalytic Review* 65 (1978): 253–79.

Politzer, Heinz. "The Alienated Self: A Key to Franz Kafka's *Castle*?" *Michigan Quarterly Review* 14 (1975): 398–414.

———. *Franz Kafka: Parable and Paradox*. Ithaca: Cornell University Press, 1966.

Priestley, J. B. "Kafka: The Last Irony: *The Castle*." *The Sunday Times,* 7 February 1954.

Reed, Eugene E. "Moral Polarity in Kafka's *Der Prozeß* and *Das Schloß*." *Monatshefte* 46 (1954): 317–24.

Robert, Marthe. *As Lonely as Franz Kafka*. Translated by Ralph Manheim. New York: Schocken, 1986.

———. *The Old and the New: From Kafka to Don Quixote*. Berkeley and Los Angeles: University of California Press, 1977.

Robertson, Ritchie. *Kafka: Judaism, Politics, and Literature*. Oxford: Clarendon, 1985.

Rolleston, James. *Kafka's Narrative Theater*. University Park: Pennsylvania State University Press, 1974.

Sheppard, Richard. *On Kafka's* Castle. New York: Barnes & Noble, 1977.

Sizemore, Christine W. "Cognitive Dissonance and the Anxiety of Response to Kafka's *The Castle*." *Comparatist* 4 (1980): 23–30.

Slochower, Harry. *A Franz Kafka Miscellany*. New York: Twice a Year Press, 1946.

Sokel, Walter. *Franz Kafka*. New York: Columbia University Press, 1966.

Spann, Meno. *Franz Kafka*. Boston: Twayne, 1976.

Spilka, Mark. *Dickens and Kafka: A Mutual Interpretation*. Bloomington: Indiana University Press, 1963.

Stern, J. P., ed. *The World of Franz Kafka*. New York: Holt, Rinehart & Winston, 1980.

Stern, J. P., and J. J. White, eds. *Paths and Labyrinths*. London: Institute of Germanic Studies, 1985.

Sussman, Henry. *Franz Kafka: Geometrician of Metaphor*. Madison, Wis.: Coda Press, 1979.

Tauber, Herbert. *Franz Kafka*. New Haven: Yale University Press, 1948.

Thorlby, Anthony. *Kafka: A Study*. London: Heinemann, 1972.

Tiefenbrun, Ruth. *Moment of Torment*. Carbondale: Southern Illinois University Press, 1973.

Urzidil, Johannes. *There Goes Kafka*. Detroit: Wayne State University Press, 1968.

Webster, Peter Dow. "A Critical Examination of Franz Kafka's *The Castle*." *American Imago* 8 (1951): 3–28.

Weinberg, Helen. *The New Novel in America: The Kafkan Mode in Contemporary Fiction*. Ithaca: Cornell University Press, 1970.

West, Rebecca. *The Court and the Castle*. New Haven: Yale University Press, 1957.

Wilson, Edmund. "A Dissenting Opinion on Franz Kafka." In *Classics and Commercials*. New York: Farrar, Straus, 1950.

Winkelman, John. "An Interpretation of Kafka's *Das Schloss*." *Monatshefte* 64 (1972): 115–31.

Zyla, Wolodymyr, ed. *Franz Kafka: His Place in World Literature*. Lubbock: The Texas Tech Press, 1971.

Acknowledgments

"The Caricature of Courtship" (originally entitled "The Caricature of Courtship: Kafka [*The Castle*]") by Kenneth Burke from *A Rhetoric of Motives* by Kenneth Burke, pages 233–44, notes and first sentence have been deleted, © 1969 by Kenneth Burke. Reprinted by permission of the University of California Press. All translations of *Das Schloss* are by Willa and Edwin Muir.

"The Undiscover'd Country: The Death Motif in Kafka's *Castle*" by W. G. Sebald from *Journal of European Studies* 2, no. 1 (March 1972), © 1972 by Science History Publications Ltd. Reprinted by permission. All translations of *Das Schloss* are taken from the Penguin edition.

"*The Castle:* To Deny Whatever Is Affirmed" (originally entitled "*The Castle*") by Ronald Gray from *Franz Kafka* by Ronald Gray, © 1973 by Cambridge University Press. Reprinted by permission of Cambridge University Press and the author. All translations of *Das Schloss* are by Willa and Edwin Muir.

"*The Castle:* A Company of Gnostic Demons" (originally entitled "*The Castle*") by Erich Heller from *Kafka* by Erich Heller, © 1974 by Erich Heller. Reprinted by permission of William Collins Sons & Co., Ltd. All translations of *Das Schloss*are by Willa and Edwin Muir.

"Power and Authority in *The Castle*" by Richard J. Arneson from *Mosaic* 12, no. 4 (Summer 1979), © 1979 by the University of Manitoba Press. Reprinted by permission. All translations of *Das Schloss* are by Willa and Edwin Muir.

"Texts, Textuality, and Silence in Franz Kafka's *The Castle*" (originally entitled "Texts, Textuality, and Silence in Franz Kafka's *Das Schloss*") by Marjanne E. Goozé from *MLN* 98, no. 3 (April 1983), © 1983 by The Johns Hopkins University Press, Baltimore/London. Reprinted by permission of the Johns Hopkins University Press. All translations of *Das Schloss, Der Prozess,* and "Das Schweigen der Sirenen" are by Willa and Edwin Muir. The translation of the passage from "Er" is by Christina Büchmann.

All excerpts from *The Castle, Definitive Edition* by Franz Kafka, translated by Willa and Edwin Muir, © 1958, by Alfred A. Knopf, Inc. are reprinted by permission of Alfred A. Knopf, Inc.

Index

Adorno, Theodore, on Schubert's
works, 36, 37, 42
Allegory(ies): *The Castle* as religious,
84, 93, 96; names of characters
interpreted as, 93–94, 135; symbol
versus, 88; women's sexual repression as religious, 135
Amalia: denial of Castle's authority by,
117, 131, 136–37; Frieda's hostility
toward, 53, 63; K.'s attitude toward, 117–18, 137, 138–39; parents of, 40–41; personality of, 62;
rejection of Sortini by, 40, 53,
100, 113; and refusal to interpret
texts, 125, 133, 135, 139–40; significance of dress worn by, 40;
silence of, 138, 139, 140; Sortini's
letter to, 27, 64, 117, 127, 130,
134
Amerika, 43
Angelus Novus (Benjamin), 43
Arthur, 38, 115
Authority: civil, 124; Kafka's spiritual,
12; political, 122, 124. *See also*
Power and authority

Barnabas, 41, 95, 126; allegory relating
to name of, 93–94; importance to
K. of, 131–32; family of, 44, 111;
mystery of, 29; personality of, 62
Beckett, Samuel, 35
Bells: meaning of ringing of, 75; ring-
ing of castle, 43, 61
Benjamin, Walter, 37, 43, 48
Blake, William, 2, 13
Boyg (*Peer Gynt*), 23

Bridge Inn. *See* Brückenhof
Brod, Max, 2, 28, 68, 135; completion
of *The Castle* by, 80; on Kafka and
Kierkegaard, 32, 63; and Kafka on
Gnosticism, 1
Brückenhof, 43, 47; Frieda and K. at,
62
Brunelda (*America*), 43
Brunswick, Hans, 45, 77; on K.'s visit
to his mother, 67
Bunyan, John, 96
Bürgel, 52, 129; allegory relating to
name of, 94; interview between K.
and, 45–46, 68–72, 73, 74, 76,
103–4, 118–19, 123, 139, 140; time
spent in bed by, 39
Burgomaster of Riva ("The Hunter
Gracchus"), 6
"Burrow, The," 66
Bürstner, Fräulein, (*The Trial*), 43, 61

"Cares of a Family Man, The," 9
Carlyle, Thomas, 13
Castiglione, Baldassare, 26; *The Courtier,* 24, 27, 29
Castle, 28; behavior of officials in, 26,
74–75; description of, 60; as hierarchic principle, 30; human qualities of, 55; identification of God
with, 107–8; K.'s antagonism toward, 100; K.'s attempt to penetrate, 37, 75–76, 79; K.'s
comparison of his home with, 41–
42, 47; as image of death, 38, 43–
44, 48; landscape surrounding,
36–37, 38; meaning of word for,

Castle (*continued*)
30; organization of, 52, 57, 61; as a political authority, 122–24; ringing of bell from, 43, 61; significance of telephone in, 56; spiritual nature of, 55–56; as symbol of power and authority, 85, 108, 116–17, 123–24; villagers and, 109, 110, 121–22, 124

Castle, The: allegorical elements in, 84, 93; analogy between *Tonio Kröger* and, 24; as autobiographical novel, 18; comparison of *The Trial* with, 52–53, 54, 60, 61–62, 68; education theme in, 29, 30; evaluation of, 21–22; final chapter of, 77; Gnostic nature of, 12, 18, 19, 99–101; hierarchy among characters in, 57, 78, 110; interrelationship of characters in, 52–53; Kierkegaardian interpretation of, 107; laughter themes in, 29; Manichaean nature of, 102, 104; mysticism in, 26, 55–56, 69–70, 73; Nietzschean interpretation of, 107–8; political interpretation of, 109, 111–24; references to weariness in, 31; as a religious parable, 107–8; role of conscious mind in writing of, 52, 53; signs of Kafka's illness in, 31–32; as a symbolic novel, 84, 88; as an unfinished novel, 52, 80; word use in, 65–68

Catholicism, 12, 28

Chaplin, Charlie, 38, 74

Childishness: in Frieda's and K.'s lovemaking, 31; in K.'s behavior, 115; reflected in the Castle, 30

Class: courtship and, 23–24; importance of, to village characters, 110; K.'s confrontation with hierarchy of, 29; mystery and, 27–28; sexual affection and, 112, 113

Complete Stories, The, 92, 97

Cordovero, Moses, 5

Count Westwest (*The Castle*), 58, 100

Courtier, The (Castiglione), 24, 27, 29

Courtship, 23–24, 29

Crow(s) (kafkas): assault on frontiers by, 4; definition of, 2; Gracchus as, 6; Josephine as, 16; K. as, 19

Dante, 9, 17

Dearest Father, 82

Death: Castle as the image of, 38, 43–44, 48; K.'s proximity to, 48–49, 79, 80; landscape of the Castle and, 47–48; sleep relationship to, 38–39; Sortini as a harbinger of, 39

de Leon, Moses, 5

Demiurge, 1, 19

Derrida, Jacques, 13

Description of a Struggle, 101

Diaries of Kafka: dialectical adoption of negative in, 13; meditation on a "breakdown" in, 2; on memory, 17; on pit of Babel, 73; reference to touching feet of a corpse in, 47

Doubtful Guest, The, (Gorey), 10

Duino Elegies (Rilke), 49, 57, 83

Education, as theme in *The Castle,* 29, 30

Elisha Ben Abuyah, 15

Emrich, Wilhelm, 53, 139; identification of Klamm as Eros by, 19–21; on name Odradek, 10

Endgame (Beckett), 41

Erlanger, 52, 72, 73; allegory relating to name of, 94; on Castle's treatment of villagers, 121–22

Eros, Herr Klamm identified as, 19–20, 21

Faust II (Goethe), 88

Fear and Trembling (Kierkegaard), 32, 63

Four Zoas, The (Blake), 13

Frank, Jacob, 4, 15

Franz Kafka: Der Künstler (Politzer), 137

Freud, Sigmund, 31; death drive of, 11; discourse of Shakespeare by, 2; "frontier concept" of, 4; *An Outline of Psychoanalysis,* 19; repression theory of, 7; theory of identity of life and death wish of, 42; version of negative by, 9, 13

Frieda: allegory relating to name of, 94; and desire to leave village with

K., 49, 138; hostility toward Amalia of, 53, 63; K.'s changing attitude toward, 112, 113; K.'s comparison of Pepi and, 78, 120–21; K.'s love for, 98–99; Klamm and, 21, 39, 121; on love, 54; personality of, 61–62; seductiveness of, 27; sexual relations between K. and, 20–21, 28, 42–43, 101; superiority in appearance of, 57

Gardena (landlady of Brückenhof), 43; description of, 57; relationship between Klamm and, 62, 112, 131
Genesis, 33
Gerstäcker, 43, 49, 61, 80
Gisa, 135
Gnosticism, 1; explanation of, 2; Kafka and, 13, 83–84; the Law and, 15; literary, 12; representation of, in *The Castle*, 12, 18, 19, 99–101
Goethe, Johann Wolfgang von: *Faust II*, 88; *Maximen und Reflexionen*, 88; *Torquato Tasso*, 91
Gorey, Edward, 10
Gracchus ("The Hunter Gracchus"): Kafka as, 8; as a crow, 6–7
Grandmother, The (Němcová), 55
Gray, Ronald, 48–49
Great Wall of China, The, 53, 82, 96
Greenberg, Martin, 19
Grillparzer, Franz, 91

Halevi, Judah, 5, 14
Hans. *See* Brunswick, Hans
Hegel, Georg Wilhelm: on alienation of man, 69; version of the Negative by, 9, 13
Heidegger, Martin, version of the Negative by, 9, 13
Heller, Erich: on Gnostic nature of *The Castle*, 12; interpretation of the Castle by, 18; on Kafka's evasiveness, 5; on love affair between K. and Frieda, 21; on women's sexual repression, 135
Herrenhof: landlady of, 48, 114–15; as symbol of the underworld, 47–48
Hesse, Hermann, 53

Hierarchy, 12; among characters in *The Castle*, 57, 78, 110; castle and, 30; social, 29; village, 110
Hölderlin, Friedrich, 80, 91
Huld (*The Trial*), 66
Hunger Artist, A, 31
"Hunter Gracchus, The," 8, 9, 49

"Imperial Message, An," 8–9
Ingeborg (*Tonio Kröger*), 23
In the Gallery, 44
"In the Penal Colony," 66, 76

Jackdaw. *See* Crow
Jackson, Shirley, 31
Jeremiah, 38, 115
Jesenská, Milena: on Kafka and *kenoma*, 1, 2; relationship between Kafka and, 52
Jewish tradition: interpretation of, 5, 7–8; Kafka on meaning of, 8–9
Josephine ("Josephine the Singer, or the Mouse Folk"), 16–17
"Josephine the Singer, or the Mouse Folk," 14, 66; doubts about writing in, 59
Joseph K. (*The Trial*), comparison of K. with, 53, 59, 71, 77, 130–31
Joyce, James, 9, 84
Judaism: eclecticism of, 12; the Law and, 13, 14–15; the Negative in, 13

K.: assistants of, 38, 60, 115; attempts to reach the Castle by, 37, 75–76, 79; attitude toward Amalia by, 117–18, 137, 138–39; attitude toward the Castle by, 43–44, 100, 109, 111, 114, 117, 118, 122, 130; changing attitude toward Frieda by, 112, 113; childish behavior of, 115; comparison of Joseph K. and, 53, 59, 71, 77, 130–31; comparison of Pepi with Frieda by, 78, 120–21; dismissal of case against, 74, 75; efforts to meet Klamm by, 19, 27, 52, 58, 114–16, 130; Frieda's desire to leave village

K.: (*continued*)
with, 49, 138; healing power of,
45; on ignorance, 53; interpretation of letter from Klamm by,
126–27, 131–32; interview
between Bürgel and, 45–46, 68–
72, 73, 74, 76, 103–4, 118–19,
123, 139, 140; involvement in village hierarchy by, 110; landlady of
Herrenhof and, 36, 114–15; love
for Frieda, 98–99; messianic traits
of, 44, 45; Pepi as personification
of ambition of, 102–3; personality
of, 61, 78, 79, 110, 111; and proximity to death, 48–49, 79, 80; reaction to family of Barnabas by,
111; reference to "indestructible
peace" by, 73, 75; rejection of
Frieda's wish to leave by, 49, 138;
relation between Pepi and, 73, 78,
79, 119, 130; representation of
Kafka by, 29, 44, 93; respect for
official papers by, 128, 129, 130;
sexual relations between Frieda
and, 20–21, 28, 42–43, 101; as a
surveyor, 18, 36, 59–60, 93, 94–
95; truth and illusion as bases of
beliefs of, 95; vision of, upon entering village, 3
Kabbalah: Kafkan perspective of a
new, 2, 5, 13, 18, 22; Zionism
and, 3, 4
Kafka. *See* Crow
Kafka, Franz: anti-Semitism and, 24;
and attempt to continue unfinished
manuscript of Castle, 105; beast
fables of, 9; belief in Absolute
Truth of, 96; on creation of
Frieda, 62; curse evident in novels
of, 82–83, 86, 87; desire for death
by, 36; emphasis on Jewishness of,
17, 47; evasion of interpretation
by, 5, 9, 14, 35; Gnosticism of, 1,
13, 83–84; on identity of life and
death wish, 42; illness of, 31–32,
51; images of death in work of,
35, 36; and images of truth, 81–
82; on the indestructible, 73; interpretation of Torah by, 8;
inventiveness and originality of, 9;

irrationality in writing of, 64–65;
literary versus spiritual authority
of, 12; Milena Jesenská and, 1, 2,
52; on morality, 108–9; new Kabbalah of, 2, 5, 13, 18, 22; Nietzsche's influence on, 86–87; oppressive atmosphere of novels of, 82,
96; "out" intellectual class of, 30;
parables of, 8–9, 14–17; preoccupied with Evil, 102; relations between father and, 31, 85–86;
religious motivation of, 26, 28,
85, 107; repetitious use of words
by, 65–67; spiritual authority of,
12; study of law by, 32; symbolic
nature of work of, 92–93; Thomas
Mann on, 23–24; treatment of
courtship by, 23, 24, 29; treatment
of mystery by, 24–25, 26, 27, 29;
unsexiness of male characters in
novels of, 43; use of metaphors
by, 4; version of Negative by, 2,
9, 11, 13, 14, 16, 21–22; women
in novels of, 43; writing style of,
65–68; and Zionism, 14
"Kafka's Cage" (Stallman), 32
Kafka-Symposion (Wagenbach), 52
Kenoma: description of, 1; Gnosticism
and, 2; K. and, 3; Klamm and,
18
Kierkegaard, Søren Aabye: "Fear and
Trembling," 32, 63; interpretation
of *The Castle* by, 107; interpretation of Genesis by, 33; "Repetition," 37
Klamm, Herr, 18, 65, 68, 95; attachment of women to, 62, 63; comparison of an eagle and, 54;
description of, 19, 57, 58; Frieda
and, 21, 39, 121; identified with
Eros, 19–20, 21; K.'s efforts to
meet, 19, 27, 52, 58, 114–16, 130;
K.'s interpretation of letter from,
126–27; K.'s oral message to, 131–
32; meaning of name of, 30–31,
58, 93; power over K. of, 27, 28;
and relations between K. and
Frieda, 21, 28; things done in
name of, 28
Kleist, Heinrich von, 91

Klopstock, Robert, 8
Komensky, Jan Amos, 55

Labyrinth of the World and the Paradise of the Heart, The (Komensky), 55
Landlady of the Brückenhof. *See* Gardena
Landlady of the Herrenhof: dresses of, 48; K. and, 36, 114–15
Lasemann, 41
Law: in Judaism, 14–15; positive versus theologic, 32
Leni (*The Trial*), 43, 62
Leverkühn, Adrian (*Doctor Faustus*), 39–40, 43
"Little Fable, A," 97
Lizaverta (*Tonio Kröger*), 24
Luria, Isaac, 4, 5
Luther, Martin, 90

Macbeth (Shakespeare), 13
Maimonides, 5
Manichaean beliefs, 99, 101, 104
Mann, Thomas, 28, 91; analogy between *The Castle* and *Toni Kröger* by, 23–24; *Tristan,* 32
Marriage of Heaven and Hell, The (Blake), 16
Maximen and Reflexionen (Goethe), 88
Mayor, the, 62, 122; description of Castle officials by, 114, 123; description of Sortini's office by, 129; interpretation of letters to K. by, 127
Metamorphosis, The, 31, 53, 66
Metaphors, Kafka's use of, 3, 4
Mills, John Stuart, 109
Milton, John, 17
Minima Moralia (Adorno), 42
Mirandola, Pico della, 90
Mizzi, 127, 128
Moments Musicaux (Adorno), 36
Momus, 44, 52, 128; allegory relating to name of, 94; indictment of K. written by, 98
Mother Courage (Brecht), 37

Mystery: laughter and, 29; officialdom and, 26, 27; relation between class and, 27–28
Mysticism, 69–70, 73

Nag (*Endgame*), 41
Nathan of Gaza, Kabbalah of, 4, 5, 15
Negative, the: Judaism and, 13; Kafka's version of, 2, 9, 11, 13, 14, 16, 21–22
Nell (*Endgame*), 41
Němcová, Božena, 55
Nietzsche, Friedrich Wilhelm, 5, 9, 91, 105, 107–8; as influence on Kafka, 86; *Übermensch,* 87; *The Will to Power,* 87

Odradek ("The Cares of a Family Man"), 9; interpretation of, 10–11; Kafka's version of Negation in, 11; meaning of name of, 10
Oedipus complex, 85
Olga: description of parents by, 40–41, 66; interpretation of Sortini's letter to Amalia by, 127; K. as a hero to, 44; as object of irony, 64–65; personality of, 62; reaction to Amalia's rejection of Sortini by, 135; story of Amalia and Sortini related by, 39, 63–64, 113, 130, 133–34, 136
"On Parables," 92
Outline of Psychoanalysis, An (Freud), 19

Parable: message from God as, 8–9; problem of law as, 14–16
Pawel, Ernst, 14
Peer Gynt (*Peer Gynt*), 23
Pepi, 43, 57; K. as a hero to, 44; K.'s relations with, 73, 78, 79; as personification of K.'s ambition, 102–3; self-regard of, 77; on winter landscape, 36
Philippi, Klaus-Peter, 139
Pilgrim's Progress (Bunyan), 84
Plato, 81

Politzer, Heinz, 39, 58; on Amalia, 138; *Franz Kafka: Der Künstler,* 137; on Kafka and Nietzsche, 9
Power and authority theme: relating to Castle, 85, 108, 122–24; sexual relations related to, 111–12, 113
Problem of Our Laws, The, 14
Prometheus legends, 87
Protestantism, 27–28
Proust, Marcel, 9, 48

Reality: the arts and, 91; society based on model of, 89–90; symbolic significance of, 88–89
"Reflections on Sin, Pain, Hope, and the True Way," 2, 82, 97
Reflexion und Wirklichkeit (Philippi), 139
Religion: *The Castle* and, 108; Gnosticism as, 2; of Kafka, 26, 28, 85, 107; parables and, 8–9; politics and, 109
Repetition (Kierkegaard), 38
Republic (Plato), 81
"Requiem" (Rilke), 89
Rilke, Rainer Maria, 79; *Duino Elegies,* 49, 57, 83; "Requiem," 89
Rimbaud, Arthur, 11
Road through the Wall, The (Jackson), 31
Rossmann, Karl, 38

St. Teresa of Avila, 55–56
Sappho (Grillparzer), 91
Sartor Resartus (Carlyle), 13
Scholem, Gershom, 1, 15; combination of Kabbalah and Zionism by, 3, 4; Kabbalah of, 4, 5, 13; Kafka's influence on, 2
Schopenhauer, Arthur, 71, 72
Schubert, Franz, song cycles of, 36, 37, 42
Schulz, Bruno, 45
Schwarzer, 38, 135
Shakespeare, William, 85, 100; Freud on, 2; *Macbeth,* 13
Sokel, Walter, 135
Sortini, 32, 68; Amalia's rejection of, 40, 53, 63, 100, 113; as envoy of

death, 39; letter to Amalia from, 27, 64, 117, 127, 130, 134
Spinoza, Baruch, 5
Stallman, R. W., 32
Strauss, Leo, 5
Strindberg, August, 98
Superintendent, the, 56, 79; on Castle organization, 57; as object of irony, 64, 65
Symbol: allegory versus, 88; *The Castle* and, 88; Goethe and, 92; Kafka and, 92–93; reality and, 88–89; sacramental, 90

Talmud: interpretation of Jewish tradition by, 7–8; as message from the distance, 8–9
Tasso (Goethe), 91
Teacher, the, 42, 100, 128
"Temptation in the Village," 52
Texts (in *The Castle*): Amalia's refusal to interpret, 125, 139–40; reader's interpretation of, 126, 133, 140; as representative of Castle's authority, 125
Textuality, 125, 126
Thus Spake Zarathustra (Nietzsche), 86
Titorelli (*The Trial*), 55, 62, 66
Tonio (*Tonio Kröger*), 23, 24
Tonio Kröger (Mann), 23, 24, 91
Torah, 7, 15; Kafka's interpretation of, 8
Trial, The, 59, 102; comparison of *The Castle* with, 52–53, 54, 60, 61–62, 68
Tristan (Mann), 32

Übermensch (Nietzsche), 87

Van den Berg, J. H., 7
von der Vogelweide, Walter, 49
von Regensburg, Berthold, 43

Wagenbach, Klaus, 36, 47, 52
Will to Power, The (Nietzsche), 87
Women: courtliness in terms of, 27; K.'s relations with, 131; in Kafka's novels, 43; sexual relations be-

tween officials and village, 135; village documents and, 130

Yahweh, 1–2, 10; authority of, 12

Zionism: Kabbalah and, 3, 4; Kafka's interest in, 14
Zvi, Sabbatai, 4, 15
Zwingli, Huldreich, 90